THE
HOLIDAY
COOKBOOK

THE
HOLIDAY
COOKBOOK

JENI WRIGHT

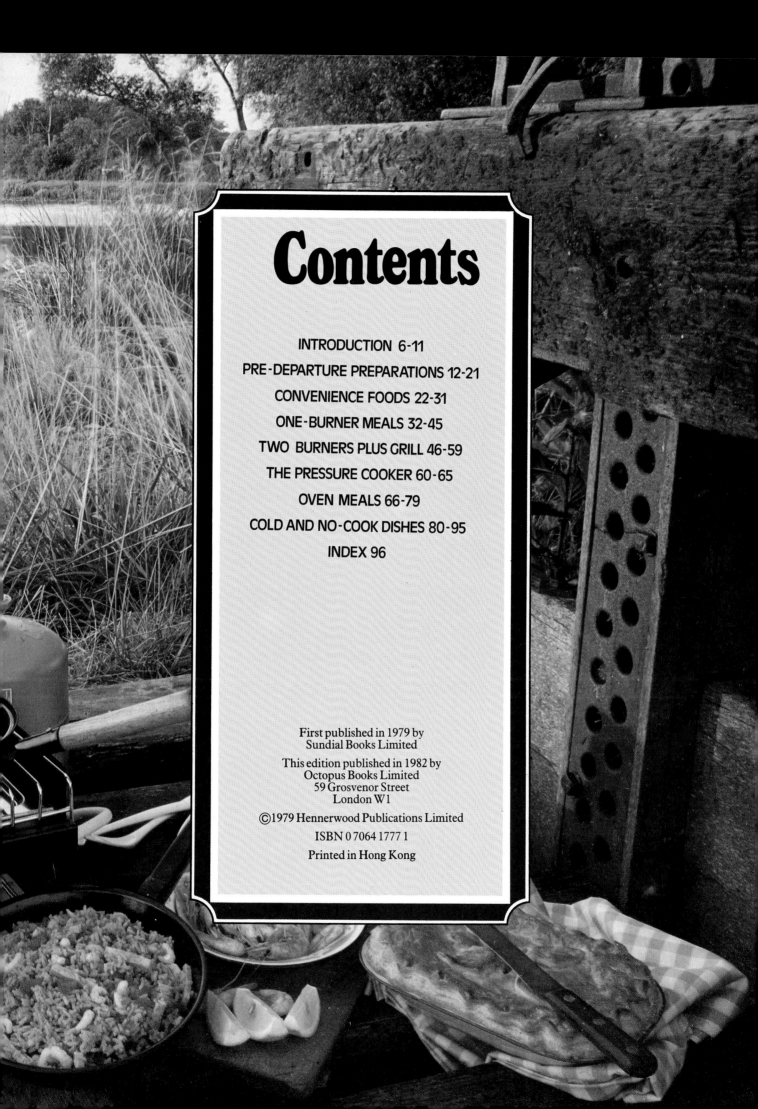

Contents

First published in 1979 by
Sundial Books Limited

This edition published in 1982 by
Octopus Books Limited
59 Grosvenor Street
London W1

©1979 Hennerwood Publications Limited

ISBN 0 7064 1777 1

Printed in Hong Kong

INTRODUCTION

When choosing the cooking equipment for your holiday, you will have to take into consideration the availability of space in your tent, caravan or boat, the number of people to be fed, and the kind of meals you will want to cook.

Cooking equipment

If you have very limited space and only want to cook simple, light meals, then you will most likely need a *single burner*. This will be light and compact for travelling – ideal if you are camping in a smallish tent. A single burner can also provide an excellent additional cooking facility if your caravan or boat is only fitted with a small cooker; and it is immensely useful to take with you on picnics, hikes and drives away from the site or mooring. There is a wide choice of single burners on the market, but the best kinds are those which incorporate a stabilizer, windshield and support grid – these are usually high pressure appliances which screw straight on to a gas cylinder.

A *double burner* is well worth the extra expense if you have room to accommodate one, not only because it will increase your cooking repertoire considerably, but also because it will make your holiday meals less of a juggling exercise and more of a pleasure! Double burners are quite sophisticated pieces of equipment, with individual knobs giving precise control. The burners are fast working, and low pressure regulators ensure even cooking with a constant flame. If you are planning to move around on holiday, the best model to choose is the folding kind which packs away into a briefcase shape for easy carrying and stacking away when not in use. When choosing a double burner, look also for good design features such as all-over grids for pan support, which are removable for easy cleaning, and built-in windshields.

If you are planning to do a lot of cooking on holiday and want to provide your family and friends with meals that are on a par with those they are used to at home, then you will most probably go for a *double burner plus grill*. These are usually built into caravans and boats as standard equipment, but they can be used equally well as free-standing cookers on top of a table in a tent awning or in the open air. The addition of the grill is particularly useful if you are cooking for a family, because it will enable you to cook meat or fish, etc., under the grill, while simmering vegetables on the burners above. However, do bear in mind that the grill on this type of cooker is considerably smaller than that on a domestic cooker. The space for the grill pan is not only smaller widthways, but also depthways, which means that you will have to take shallow containers with you to fit under the grill. Also, although most models do incorporate a temperature control, it will obviously not be as accurate as that on a domestic grill, and you will probably find it necessary to turn the food round during grilling to ensure even browning. The temperature of the grill will also fluctuate according to the number of burners you are using at the same time. Yet, despite all these differences between the camping and the domestic grill, you will find that once you have used your camping grill a few times, you will have got to grips with its idiosyncracies and will adapt your favourite recipes to suit its limitations.

If you are spending your holiday in a caravan or boat, then it may already be fitted with an *oven* or this may be offered as an optional extra. If not, then you can fit one yourself or have one fitted if there is space available. Ovens usually come as part of a cooker which incorporates two burners and a grill, although it is possible to buy ovens as separate units. The temperature control is normally a simple switch with a choice of low, medium and high, or $\frac{1}{4}$, $\frac{1}{2}$, $\frac{3}{4}$ and full, according to the manufacturer. This, together with the fact that the oven is much smaller than the average domestic oven, will obviously mean that you cannot cook such a wide variety of dishes as you can at home. As with the camping grill, however, you will soon get the feel of the oven and be able to adjust your own recipes accordingly. Do remember, though, that the heat of the oven is likely to make the inside of a small caravan or boat rather stuffy, so avoid using it for any length of time during very hot weather. Also remember to check the gas supply – an oven will use far more gas than burners and grill.

Refrigeration

Keeping things cool is a major problem on a camping holiday and before setting off it is essential to make sure that you take with you some form of cooling box or refrigerator. The latest cooling device on the market is the *insulated jug,* which has now largely superseded the thermos or vacuum flask. Most insulated jugs will keep food cool for up to 12 hours (they can also keep food hot), and are indispensable on holiday for taking food to the beach, and on picnics, hikes, drives, etc. They are made of tough, resilient plastic and are therefore not prone to breaking like the thermos; they are also available in a wide variety of shapes and sizes.

One step further up the scale from the jug is the *cool box*. This is ideal if you are camping in a tent, especially if you are on a camp site where ice can be bought and/or the freeze packs can be left in the site freezer overnight. Cool boxes work on the principle that the frozen bag or sachet containing a special chemical is put inside the box to help keep the contents of the box cool – obviously this will work more efficiently if the food is cold when put into the box in the first place. Although these boxes do not hold nearly as much food as a refrigerator, nor will they actually make ice, they will hold essential items like butter, cheese, milk, cold drinks and salad vegetables.

Camping refrigerators fall into two main categories. Firstly, there is the free-standing portable refrigerator box. This is usually run off bottled gas, although it is possible to plug it into a 12 volt car battery or even mains electricity. The distinction between this type of box and the cool box previously discussed is that while the cool box can only keep things cool for a limited period, the camping refrigerator can actually chill food and also make its own ice cubes. If you are planning on being away for a fairly long time and anticipate hot weather, it would be wise to consider investing in one of these refrigerators – even more so if you intend to go camping regularly.

The second type of refrigerator is the caravan refrigerator, which is comparable to the domestic refrigerator in all things except its size. If you are planning on travelling abroad during the summer months this type of refrigerator would be a wise investment. Many caravan manufacturers offer a built-in refrigerator as an optional extra – this is well worth considering, not only because it can keep perishable food cold and safe, but also because it can make ice cubes and keep food frozen in the ice making compartment. There is also plenty of room for chilling desserts. This type of refrigerator normally runs off bottled gas and is extremely efficient if correctly installed. Make sure that the caravan is standing on level ground, however, or the pilot light tends to go out. The refrigerator can be connected to a 12 volt car battery when the caravan is being towed; it also works off mains electricity.

General equipment

Be careful to keep your cooking equipment down to a minimum because, apart from the obvious difficulty of transporting it, you will probably also find a distinct lack of storage space when you arrive at your destination.

Essentials

Non-stick compact cooking set (stacking pans which incorporate saucepans, frying pan, cake tins, poacher, handles, etc)
Large (25 cm/10 inch) heavy-duty non-stick frying pan
Kettle
Tea pot
Sieve or colander (preferably metal)
Wooden spoons and spatulas
Slotted spoon
Fish slice
Can and bottle opener
Corkscrew
Rotary beater or whisk
Grater (for cheese, breadcrumbs, etc)
Knives (for peeling, slicing and carving [serrated-edge])
Scissors
Bread board (use also as a chopping board)
Automatic chopper
Measuring spoons
Measuring jug (heatproof) *instead of kitchen scales*
Mixing bowls (rigid polythene with lids – to use also as storage bowls)
Salt and pepper mills
Plastic milk bottle cap
Melamine crockery
Cutlery
Silver foil and cling film
Kitchen paper towels
Insulated jug, flask or cool box (with freeze packs if necessary)
Matches
Gas lighter

Useful extras

Pressure cooker (plus spares)
Rolling pin
Baking sheet (for use with oven)
Vegetable peeler or brush
Pie dish (flameproof metal or Pyrex)
Casserole dish (large flameproof)
Loaf tin
Triple pan set (3 triangular saucepans that fit together)
Pyramid toaster (for use over burners if no grill)
Potato masher
Scoop (for ice cream or potato)
Potato baker (metal spikes for quick conduction of heat)
Plastic egg box
Insulated butter dish
Spatter screen (also useful as a strainer/cake rack, etc)
Cooker hood (fitted in caravan or boat to expel strong smells and steam)
Barbecue (preferably portable, with charcoal and firelighters)
Disposable paper cups and plates

Fuel for cooking

Bottled gas or liquefied petroleum gas (lpg) is the most common kind of fuel used with cooking appliances, and it is most likely to be butane gas that you will use. Propane gas is normally only used at high altitudes or in cold climates. Methylated spirits and paraffin were once popular for cooking, but have become less popular since the widespread distribution of bottled gas – they tend to taint the food with their strong smells and can also be dangerous and difficult to use and store. Bottled gas comes in disposable cartridges or refillable cylinders of varying sizes. In general, it is only the smaller appliances that will work off the cartridges, therefore if you are planning to cook with bottled gas, check before going away that you will be able to refill your cylinders. If not, then try to take as many with you as you think you will need (as a rough guide, all the recipes in this book were tested using two 2.72 kg (6 lb) cylinders).

In terms of intensity of flame, bottled gas gives much the same performance as domestic gas, although it must be remembered that if more than one burner is lit, this will affect the performance of the others, and the oven will use far more gas than the burners on top of the stove. Whichever make of gas you choose to use, it is absolutely essential to follow the manufacturer's instructions for connecting the gas to appliances and for changing a cartridge or cylinder. Remember to take with you all fixing and operating instructions, also a spare hose, pressure regulator and gas spanner.

Safety first

When cooking in confined spaces and using bottled gas, it is essential to take certain safety precautions. Always keep a fire extinguisher near the cooker and an asbestos mat or cloth to dampen flames if a pan of fat should accidentally catch alight. Cookers should never be left unattended and the gas should be securely turned off at the supply when not in use. Include a first aid kit amongst your packing and make sure it is near at hand as soon as you arrive at your destination.

Suggestions for the store cupboard

When you have planned your holiday meals, then you can start collecting together the food you will need to take for your store cupboard. This will avoid endless trips to the shops while on holiday – all you should have to buy will be fresh meat and fish, fruit, vegetables and dairy produce. This list includes some of the store cupboard items necessary to make the recipes in this book. Obviously you will not want to take all of them, but it will provide you with a useful checklist.

Packets
Biscuits
Blancmange powder
Breadcrumbs (golden)
Crumble mix
Custard powder (instant)
Dehydrated vegetables (carrots, peas, etc)
Dessert mixes
Dumpling mix
Jelly cubes
Jelly glaze
Pancake and batter mix
Pastry mix
Pizza mix
Potato mix (instant)
Sauce mixes (cheese, herb, onion, parsley, white)
Savoury rice
Soups
Stuffing mix

Preserves
Golden syrup
Honey
Jam
Marmalade
Mincemeat

Herbs and spices
Allspice, basil or oregano, cinnamon, cayenne pepper, chilli powder, dried mixed herbs, ginger, mixed spice, paprika pepper, tarragon

Flavourings and sauces, etc.
Curry paste
French dressing (ready-prepared)
Garlic
Horseradish (bottled)
Lemon juice
Mayonnaise (bottled)
Mustard (dry and prepared)
Oil
Peppercorns
Salt
Sauces (soy, Tabasco, tomato ketchup, Worcestershire)
Stock cubes (beef and chicken)
Tomato purée
Wine vinegar

Cans
Fish (anchovies, mackerel, pilchards, salmon, sardines, tuna)
Fruit (apricots, mandarins, peaches, pie filling, pineapple, plums, raspberries, strawberries)
Meat (chopped ham, corned beef, frankfurters, ham, meat loaf, meatballs, minced beef, stewing steak)
Soup (condensed and regular)
Vegetables (baked beans, carrots, peas, potatoes, sweetcorn, tomatoes)

All spoon measures are level.
All eggs are grade 3, 4, 5 (standard).
Metric and imperial measures have been calculated separately. Follow one column only, they are not interchangeable.
All imperial packet and can sizes have been rounded down and metric measures adjusted to correspond. Dry ingredients have been measured in a multi-purpose measuring jug instead of on kitchen scales.

All recipes have been tested in normal kitchen conditions, using the equipment described. If you intend to make these recipes at home using a conventional oven and hob, remember that the cooking times will vary from those given here.

PRE-DEPARTURE PREPARATIONS

If you have the foresight and time to plan your holiday meals before you actually go away, then you will find shopping and cooking on holiday far less of a problem than expected. This way, you will also be sure of only taking food with you that you know you will use. Storage space is always at a premium, therefore you cannot afford to take anything with you that is not going to be used.

There are several ways in which you can prepare for your holiday before you actually depart. It helps to spend some time baking on the days immediately before your departure. Cakes and biscuits are always welcome on holiday; they help to stave off hunger in between meals, and they are essential if you have to cater for children's teas. All the baked goods in this chapter will keep well and the rich fruit cakes even improve with age. If possible, make cakes in square tins for easy stacking and storage, and wrap all food well in silver foil or cling film before packing in airtight containers.

Well-seasoned campers advocate preparing a complete meal or two before setting off. This saves time and energy both en route and on arrival at your destination, when it is sometimes difficult to set up cooking equipment quickly. The two main course suggestions in this chapter travel well and their flavours are enhanced by keeping. Transfer them straight from their cooking dishes to insulated jugs or flasks where they should keep hot for about 4 hours; after this time you will probably have to reheat them before serving.

Cut and come again cake

Metric	Imperial
225 g self-raising flour	8 oz self-raising flour
1 × 5 ml spoon salt	1 teaspoon salt
1 × 5 ml spoon baking powder	1 teaspoon baking powder
1 × 5 ml spoon ground mixed spice	1 teaspoon ground mixed spice
225 g wholemeal flour	8 oz wholemeal flour
225 g dark soft brown sugar	8 oz dark soft brown sugar
225 g butter	8 oz butter
175 g sultanas	6 oz sultanas
175 g currants	6 oz currants
175 g seedless raisins	6 oz seedless raisins
50 g glacé cherries, quartered	2 oz glacé cherries, quartered
50 g cut mixed peel	2 oz cut mixed peel
finely grated rind and juice of 1 orange	finely grated rind and juice of 1 orange
3 × 15 ml spoons thick cut marmalade	3 tablespoons thick cut marmalade
300 ml sweet stout	½ pint sweet stout

Cooking time: 2¼ hours
Oven: 170°C, 325°F, Gas Mark 3

Sift the self-raising flour, salt, baking powder and spice into a large bowl. Stir in the wholemeal flour and sugar, then rub in the butter with the fingertips. Add the dried fruit, cherries and peel, orange rind, juice and marmalade. Stir well to mix, then stir in enough sweet stout to give a soft dropping consistency. Spoon the mixture into a greased deep 20 cm/8 inch square cake tin lined with greased greaseproof paper and smooth the top. Bake just below the centre of a preheated moderate oven for 2¼ hours until a skewer inserted in the centre comes out clean. Cover with foil if the cake becomes too brown during baking.
Leave to cool in the tin then remove the greaseproof paper. Wrap in foil, overwrap in a polythene bag and store in an airtight container.
Makes 24 slices

Sticky date gingerbread

Metric	Imperial
225 g butter	8 oz butter
225 g dark soft brown sugar	8 oz dark soft brown sugar
100 g golden syrup	4 oz golden syrup
100 g black treacle	4 oz black treacle
500 g flour	1 lb flour
1 × 15 ml spoon ground ginger	1 tablespoon ground ginger
2 × 5 ml spoons ground cinnamon	2 teaspoons ground cinnamon
2 eggs, beaten	2 eggs, beaten
150 ml milk, warmed	¼ pint milk, warmed
1½ × 5 ml spoons bicarbonate of soda	1½ teaspoons bicarbonate of soda
100 g sugar rolled chopped dates	4 oz sugar rolled chopped dates

Cooking time: 1¼ hours
Oven: 150°C, 300°F, Gas Mark 2

Gingerbread is best left to mature for several days, so make this cake one of the last you eat on holiday.

Put the butter, sugar, syrup and treacle in a pan and heat gently until melted, stirring occasionally. Remove from the heat.
Sift the flour and spices into a large bowl and make a well in the centre. Pour in the melted mixture and beat well to combine. Beat in the eggs. Mix the milk and soda together and add to the mixture with the dates.
Line the bottom of a greased roasting tin (approximately 35 × 25 cm/14 × 10 inch) with greased greaseproof paper. Pour in the mixture. Bake just below the centre of a preheated cool oven for 1¼ hours or until a skewer inserted in the centre comes out clean.
Leave to cool in the tin, then remove the greaseproof paper. Cut the gingerbread into two, wrap each half individually in foil and overwrap in polythene bags. Store in an airtight container. Serve cut into squares and spread with butter.
Makes 30 slices

From left: Cut and come again cake; Sticky date gingerbread

Banana nut bread

Metric	Imperial
225 g butter	8 oz butter
225 g caster sugar	8 oz caster sugar
2 × 15 ml spoons thick honey	2 tablespoons thick honey
4 eggs, beaten	4 eggs, beaten
500 g self-raising flour	1 lb self-raising flour
1 × 2.5 ml spoon salt	½ teaspoon salt
1 × 2.5 ml spoon bicarbonate of soda	½ teaspoon bicarbonate of soda
4 medium ripe bananas, peeled and mashed	4 medium ripe bananas, peeled and mashed
100 g walnuts, roughly chopped	4 oz walnuts, roughly chopped

Cooking time: about 1¼ hours
Oven: 180°C, 350°F, Gas Mark 4

Put the butter, sugar and honey in a bowl and beat together until light and fluffy. Beat in the eggs a little at a time, adding a little flour with each addition. Sift remaining flour, salt and soda together, then fold into the creamed mixture. Beat in the bananas and nuts. Spoon the mixture into two greased 1 kg/2 lb loaf tins lined with greased greaseproof paper. Bake just below the centre of a preheated moderate oven for 1¼ hours or until well risen and a skewer inserted in the centre comes out clean.

Leave to cool in the tin, then remove the greaseproof paper. Wrap each cake in foil, overwrap in polythene bags and store in airtight containers. Serve cut into thick slices and spread with butter, if liked.
Makes 24 slices

Tea brack

Metric	Imperial
500 g mixed dried fruit	1 lb mixed dried fruit
4 × 15 ml spoons thick honey	4 tablespoons thick honey
300 ml strained cold tea	½ pint strained cold tea
2 eggs, beaten	2 eggs, beaten
50 g butter, melted	2 oz butter, melted
2 × 15 ml spoons milk	2 tablespoons milk
500 g self-raising flour	1 lb self-raising flour

Cooking time: 1¼–1½ hours
Oven: 170°C, 325°F, Gas Mark 3

Put the fruit, honey and tea in a large bowl and stir well to mix. Cover with a cloth and leave to soak overnight. Beat in the remaining ingredients until evenly mixed, then spoon into a greased deep 18 cm/ 7 inch square cake tin lined with greased greaseproof paper.

Bake just below the centre of a preheated moderate oven for 1¼ to 1½ hours or until a skewer inserted in the centre comes out clean. Cover the top of the cake with foil if it becomes too brown during baking.

Remove it from the oven and leave to cool in the tin, then remove the greaseproof paper. Wrap in foil, overwrap in a polythene bag and store in an airtight container. Serve cut into thin slices and spread with butter.
Makes 24 slices

Almond and cherry cake

Metric	Imperial
225 g butter	8 oz butter
275 g caster sugar	10 oz caster sugar
6 eggs, beaten	6 eggs, beaten
75 g self-raising flour, sifted	3 oz self-raising flour, sifted
225 g ground almonds	8 oz ground almonds
1 × 5 ml spoon almond essence	1 teaspoon almond essence
175 g glacé cherries, washed, dried and quartered	6 oz glacé cherries, washed, dried and quartered

Cooking time: about 1¼ hours
Oven: 180°C, 350°F, Gas Mark 4

This is a moist cake which keeps very well.

Put the butter and sugar in a bowl and beat together until light and fluffy. Beat in the eggs a little at a time, adding a little flour with each addition. Coat the cherries in the flour, then fold in any remaining flour with the almonds until evenly blended. Beat in the essence and cherries. Line a greased deep 20cm/8 inch square cake tin with greased greaseproof paper, then spoon in the mixture.

Bake just below the centre of a preheated moderate oven for 1¼ hours or until a skewer inserted in the centre comes out clean. Leave to cool in the tin, then remove the greaseproof paper. Wrap in cling film, overwrap in a polythene bag and store in an airtight container.
Makes 24 slices

From front: Tea brack; Banana nut bread; Almond and cherry cake

Ginger snaps

Metric	Imperial
75 g butter	3 oz butter
75 g dark soft brown sugar	3 oz dark soft brown sugar
2 × 15 ml spoons golden syrup	2 tablespoons golden syrup
2 × 15 ml spoons black treacle	2 tablespoons black treacle
175 g self-raising flour	6 oz self-raising flour
2 × 5 ml spoons ground ginger	2 teaspoons ground ginger

Cooking time: 7–10 minutes
Oven: 180°C, 350°F, Gas Mark 4

Put the butter, sugar, syrup and treacle in a pan and heat gently until melted, stirring occasionally.
Sift the flour and ginger into a bowl, then stir in the melted mixture until the dough draws together. Put teaspoonfuls of the mixture on lightly greased baking sheets, spacing them well apart. Press down with the fingertips to form flat round shapes. Bake in a preheated moderate oven for 7 to 10 minutes.
Leave to set on the baking sheets for a few minutes, then transfer to a wire rack and leave to cool completely. Wrap neatly in foil and store in an airtight container.
Makes about 30

From left:
Spiced sultana cookies; Munchy muesli squares; Ginger snaps

Munchy muesli squares

Metric	Imperial
225 g muesli	8 oz muesli
3 × 15 ml spoons thick honey	3 tablespoons thick honey
3 × 15 ml spoons golden syrup	3 tablespoons golden syrup
50 g butter, softened	2 oz butter, softened

Cooking time: 15–20 minutes
Oven: 180°C, 350°F, Gas Mark 4

Put all the ingredients in a bowl and beat together until well mixed. Spread the mixture in a buttered 20 cm/8 inch square tin, then bake in a preheated moderate oven for 20 minutes until golden brown. Leave to cool in the tin for 5 minutes, then cut into squares and leave in the tin to cool completely. Remove the squares from the tin, wrap neatly in foil and store in an airtight container.
Makes 16

Variation:
Substitute porridge oats for the muesli.

Spiced sultana cookies

Metric	Imperial
225 g self-raising flour	8 oz self-raising flour
1 × 5 ml spoon ground mixed spice	1 teaspoon ground mixed spice
pinch of salt	pinch of salt
100 g wholemeal flour	4 oz wholemeal flour
100 g demerara sugar	4 oz demerara sugar
150 g butter	5 oz butter
1 large egg, beaten	1 large egg, beaten
50 g sultanas	2 oz sultanas
a little extra demerara sugar, for sprinkling	a little extra demerara sugar, for sprinkling

Cooking time: 10–12 minutes
Oven: 180°C, 350°F, Gas Mark 4

Sift the self-raising flour, spice and salt into a bowl. Stir in the wholemeal flour and the sugar. Rub in the butter with the fingertips, then stir in the egg to give a stiff dough.
Turn the dough out onto a floured surface and work in the sultanas with the fingertips, until evenly distributed throughout the dough. Sprinkle with plenty of flour if the dough becomes too sticky. Form into a ball, wrap in foil, then chill in the refrigerator for at least 30 minutes until firm.
Roll out small pieces of the dough on a floured surface and cut into rounds using a 5 cm/2 inch fluted biscuit cutter. Dredge the dough and surface with flour while rolling and cutting as the dough is rich and sticky.
Place on baking sheets, prick all over with a fork, then sprinkle with demerara sugar. Bake in a preheated moderate oven for 10–12 minutes until golden brown and set.
Transfer immediately to a wire rack and leave to cool. Wrap neatly in foil and store in an airtight container.
Makes 30 to 35

Muesli

Metric
1 × 225 g packet cornflakes
1 packet of 12 whole wheat
  biscuits
500 g rolled oats
350 g light soft brown
  sugar, or to taste
350 g cut mixed nuts
225 g stoned dates,
  finely chopped
500 g seedless raisins
225 g dried milk powder

Imperial
1 × 8 oz packet cornflakes
1 packet of 12 whole wheat
  biscuits
1 lb rolled oats
12 oz light soft brown
  sugar, or to taste
12 oz cut mixed nuts
8 oz stoned dates,
  finely chopped
1 lb seedless raisins
8 oz dried milk powder

Home-made muesli makes a substantial and nourish-ing quick breakfast. Make this muesli base before you go on holiday, then simply add milk, yogurt or cream and diced fresh fruit at the time of serving.

Put the cornflakes and wheat biscuits in a large bowl and crush finely with the end of a rolling pin. Stir in the remaining ingredients until evenly mixed, then transfer to an airtight container.
Makes about 24 servings

Below: Muesli

Above: Toffee treats; Vanilla fudge

Vanilla fudge

Metric
1 large can sweetened
  condensed milk
500 g light soft brown
  sugar
50 g butter
1 × 2.5 ml spoon
  vanilla essence

Imperial
1 large can sweetened
  condensed milk
1 lb light soft brown
  sugar
2 oz butter
½ teaspoon vanilla
  essence

Cooking time: 5 minutes

Put all the ingredients in a heavy-based pan and heat gently until the sugar has dissolved, stirring occasionally. Increase the heat and boil rapidly for 5 minutes, stirring constantly with a wooden spoon until the mixture becomes thick and dark.
Remove from the heat and continue stirring vigorously for 2 minutes until the mixture begins to look grainy. Pour immediately into a buttered 20 cm/8 inch square shallow tin. Leave for 5 minutes until just beginning to set, then cut into squares and leave in the tin until cold. Remove the fudge from the tin, break into squares and pack in an airtight container.
Makes about 750 g/1¾ lb

Variations :
Chopped nuts, raisins or grated chocolate can be added to the fudge if liked. Stir into the mixture after removing from the heat.

Toffee treats

Metric
500 g demerara sugar
225 g butter, cut into pieces
2 × 15 ml spoons golden
  syrup
175 g cut mixed nuts

Imperial
1 lb demerara sugar
8 oz butter, cut into pieces
2 tablespoons golden
  syrup
6 oz cut mixed nuts

Cooking time: 4–5 minutes

Put all the ingredients in a heavy pan and heat gently until the sugar has dissolved, stirring occasionally. Increase the heat and boil rapidly for 4 to 5 minutes until thick, stirring constantly with a wooden spoon. Spread immediately in a buttered Swiss roll tin (28 × 20 cm/11 × 8 inch), using a palette knife. Leave for 5 minutes until just beginning to set, then cut into squares and leave in the tin until cold. Store in an airtight container, interleaving the layers with greaseproof paper.
Makes about 750 g/1¾ lb

Beef in Guinness

Metric	Imperial
1 kg chuck steak, cut into cubes	2 lb chuck steak, cut into cubes
300 ml Guinness	½ pint Guinness
40 g flour	1½ oz flour
salt	salt
freshly ground black pepper	freshly ground black pepper
40 g dripping or lard	1½ oz dripping or lard
1 large onion, peeled and sliced	1 large onion, peeled and sliced
1 beef stock cube dissolved in 300 ml hot water	1 beef stock cube dissolved in ½ pint hot water
1 × 15 ml spoon Worcestershire sauce	1 tablespoon Worcestershire sauce
1 × 15 ml spoon soft brown sugar	1 tablespoon soft brown sugar
1 × 15 ml spoon tomato purée	1 tablespoon tomato purée
4 carrots, peeled and sliced	4 carrots, peeled and sliced
4 medium potatoes, peeled and cut into cubes	4 medium potatoes, peeled and cut into cubes

Cooking time: 2½ hours
Oven: 150°C, 300°F, Gas Mark 2

This hearty casserole is a meal in itself, so you will need no extra vegetables to serve with it. Start making it two days before your journey.

Put the meat in a bowl, pour over the Guinness and stir well. Leave to marinate overnight. The next day, strain the marinade and reserve. Coat the meat in the flour seasoned with salt and pepper. Melt the fat in a flameproof casserole, add the meat and fry briskly until browned on all sides. Remove from the casserole with a slotted spoon and set aside. Add the onion to the casserole and fry gently until golden. Return the meat to the casserole with the reserved marinade and stir well.

Add the remaining ingredients, except the potatoes, cover and cook in a preheated cool oven for 1½ hours. Taste and adjust the seasoning, add the potatoes and continue cooking for a further 45 minutes or until the meat and potatoes are tender.

To serve: if the casserole is to be served within 8 hours of making, transfer it to a vacuum flask or insulated jug and seal. Reheat the contents of the jug in a pan until hot and bubbling, about 15 minutes.
If it is to be kept any longer, cool the casserole and chill in the refrigerator. Chill the vacuum flask or insulated jug following the manufacturer's instructions. Reheat for about 30 minutes or until hot and bubbling.

Beef parcels in red wine

Metric	Imperial
4 thin slices of frying or minute steak (about 750 g)	4 thin slices of frying or minute steak (about 1½ lb)
salt	salt
freshly ground black pepper	freshly ground black pepper
½ × 100 g packet country stuffing mix	½ × 4 oz packet country stuffing mix
40 g butter	1½ oz butter
1 onion, peeled and chopped	1 onion, peeled and chopped
1 garlic clove, peeled and crushed (optional)	1 garlic clove, peeled and crushed (optional)
300 ml dry red wine	½ pint dry red wine
150 ml beef stock	¼ pint beef stock
225 g button mushrooms, to serve	8 oz button mushrooms, to serve

Cooking time: 1¼–1½ hours
Oven: 170°C, 325°F, Gas Mark 3

Beat the steak very thin, cut each slice in half and sprinkle with salt and pepper. Make the stuffing mix according to packet directions, divide it equally between the slices of meat. Roll up the meat to enclose the stuffing, then secure each parcel with wooden cocktail sticks.

Melt the butter in a flameproof casserole, add the parcels and fry gently until browned on all sides. Remove from the pan with a slotted spoon and set aside. Add the onion and garlic (if using) to the pan and fry gently until golden. Return the parcels to the pan, add the wine and stock and salt and pepper to taste.

Cover and cook in a preheated moderate oven for 1¼ to 1½ hours until the meat is tender, turning the parcels occasionally. Taste and adjust seasoning, then remove the cocktail sticks carefully.

To serve: serve in the same way as for Beef in Guinness, adding the mushrooms 15 minutes before the end of reheating time.

Beef parcels in red wine; Beef in Guinness

CONVENIENCE FOODS

With a little imagination and flair, convenience foods can save you endless preparation time, plus all the washing up and clearing away that goes with it. There is such a wide choice of cans, jars and packets available on the supermarket shelves that there is no need for your family or friends to become bored with their holiday food. The secret to remember is never to simply open up a can and serve it just the way it comes – if you follow the ideas in this chapter you will see how fresh vegetables and herbs can make all the difference to canned meat or fish for example, and how luscious sweets can be made by combining canned fruit with fresh cream. Use the ideas in this chapter as a guideline to dressing up your own favourite convenience foods.

Quick paella

Metric	Imperial
2 × 150 g packets Spanish or mixed vegetable rice	2 × 5 oz packets Spanish or mixed vegetable rice
1 large knob of butter	1 large knob of butter
1 × 500 g can pork shoulder, cut into thin strips	1 × 1 lb can pork shoulder, cut into thin strips
100 g fresh or frozen peeled prawns, defrosted	4 oz fresh or frozen peeled prawns, defrosted
½ green pepper, cored, seeded and finely chopped	½ green pepper, cored, seeded and finely chopped
½ red pepper, cored, seeded and finely chopped	½ red pepper, cored, seeded and finely chopped
freshly ground black pepper	freshly ground black pepper
1 lemon, quartered	1 lemon, quartered

Cooking time: 25 minutes

Cook the rice for 20 minutes according to packet directions. Stir in the remaining ingredients except the lemon quarters. Heat through for 5 minutes, stirring occasionally, then serve immediately with lemon quarters.

From front: Paprika beef goulash; Sweetcorn and ham chowder

Above: Quick paella

Paprika beef goulash

Metric	Imperial
2 × 15 ml spoons vegetable oil	2 tablespoons vegetable oil
1 large onion, peeled and finely chopped	1 large onion, peeled and finely chopped
1 × 15 ml spoon paprika	1 tablespoon paprika
1 green pepper, cored, seeded and finely chopped	1 green pepper, cored, seeded and finely chopped
1 red pepper, cored, seeded and finely chopped	1 red pepper, cored, seeded and finely chopped
2 × 425 g cans chunky steak in rich gravy	2 × 15 oz cans chunky steak in rich gravy
2 × 15 ml spoons tomato purée	2 tablespoons tomato purée
salt	salt
freshly ground black pepper	freshly ground black pepper
225 g button mushrooms, finely sliced	½ lb button mushrooms, finely sliced
soured cream or plain unsweetened yogurt, to serve	soured cream or plain unsweetened yogurt, to serve

Cooking time: 25 minutes

Heat the oil in a pan, add the onion and paprika and fry over gentle heat for 5 minutes, stirring occasionally.

Add the peppers and fry for 5 minutes until soft, then add the chunky steak, tomato purée and salt and pepper to taste. Stir well to mix, then cook gently for 10 minutes until hot and bubbling. Stir the mushrooms into the pan and cook for a further 5 minutes. Serve immediately with boiled rice and soured cream or yogurt handed separately.

Variation:
Canned mushrooms can be used instead of fresh ones.

Sweetcorn and ham chowder

Metric	Imperial
1 large knob of butter	1 large knob of butter
1 large onion, peeled and finely chopped	1 large onion, peeled and finely chopped
2 × 15 ml spoons flour	2 tablespoons flour
300 ml milk	½ pink milk
1 chicken stock cube dissolved in 600 ml hot water	1 chicken stock cube dissolved in 1 pint hot water
1 × 300 g can sweetcorn, drained	1 × 11 oz can sweetcorn, drained
1 × 200 g can sweetcure ham, diced	1 × 7 oz can sweetcure ham, diced
1 × 500 g can new potatoes, drained and diced	1 × 1 lb can new potatoes, drained and diced
freshly ground black pepper	freshly ground black pepper
1 × 2.5 ml spoon paprika	½ teaspoon paprika
grated Parmesan cheese, to serve	grated Parmesan cheese, to serve

Cooking time: 20–25 minutes

Melt the butter in a pan, add the onion and fry over gentle heat until golden brown, stirring occasionally. Add the flour and cook for 1 minute, stirring constantly, then gradually stir in the milk and chicken stock. Bring to the boil, then add the remaining ingredients except the cheese and half the paprika. Simmer for 10 minutes until hot and bubbling. Taste and adjust seasoning. Dust with the remaining paprika and serve with Parmesan cheese handed separately.

Variation:
Prawns can be substituted for the ham.

Mexican meatballs

Metric	Imperial
2 × 15 ml spoons vegetable oil	2 tablespoons vegetable oil
1 small onion, peeled and finely chopped	1 small onion, peeled and finely chopped
½ red pepper, cored, seeded and finely chopped	½ red pepper, cored, seeded and finely chopped
½ green pepper, cored, seeded and finely chopped	½ green pepper, cored, seeded and finely chopped
1 × 2.5 ml spoon chilli powder or to taste	½ teaspoon chilli powder, or to taste
2 × 425 g cans beef meatballs in tomato sauce	2 × 15 oz cans beef meatballs in tomato sauce
1 × 15 ml spoon wine vinegar	1 tablespoon wine vinegar
1 × 15 ml spoon soy sauce	1 tablespoon soy sauce
2 × 5 ml spoons brown sugar	2 teaspoons brown sugar
salt	salt
freshly ground black pepper	freshly ground plack pepper
plain unsweetened yogurt, to serve	plain unsweetened yogurt, to serve

Cooking time: 10 minutes

Chilli powders vary in strength, depending on the brand used. Since chilli is a strong spice it is wise to use it cautiously until you have found the degree of strength you prefer.

Heat the oil in a pan, add the vegetables and chilli powder and fry over moderate heat for 5 minutes until lightly coloured, stirring occasionally.
Add remaining ingredients, except the yogurt, and stir gently to mix. Cook over moderate heat for a further 5 minutes until bubbling. Taste and adjust seasoning, then serve immediately with yogurt swirled on top. Serve with boiled rice and a green salad.

Chunky beef with herb dumplings

Metric	Imperial
1 × 225 g packet suet dumpling mix	1 × 8 oz packet suet dumpling mix
1 × 5 ml spoon dried mixed herbs	1 teaspoon dried mixed herbs
2 × 15 ml spoons vegetable oil	2 tablespoons vegetable oil
1 large onion, peeled and finely chopped	1 large onion, peeled and finely chopped
1 × 400 g can tomatoes	1 × 14 oz can tomatoes
1 × 15 ml spoon tomato purée	1 tablespoon tomato purée
1 × 15 ml spoon Worcestershire sauce	1 tablespoon Worcestershire sauce
pinch of sugar	pinch of sugar
salt	salt
freshly ground black pepper	freshly ground black pepper
2 × 425 g cans chunky steak in rich gravy	2 × 15 oz cans chunky steak in rich gravy
1 × 275 g can carrots, drained and chopped	1 × 10 oz can carrots, drained and chopped

Cooking time: 30–35 minutes

Make 12 small dumplings according to the packet directions, adding half the dried mixed herbs to the mix before adding the water. Set aside. Heat the oil in a pan, add the onion and fry over gentle heat until soft, stirring occasionally. Add the tomatoes and break up with a spoon, then stir in the tomato purée, Worcestershire sauce, sugar, remaining herbs and salt and pepper to taste. Bring to the boil, lower the heat and add the dumplings. Cover and cook over the lowest possible heat for 15 minutes, shaking the pan occasionally. Do not stir or this will break up the dumplings.
Add the chunky steak and carrots, shaking the pan to mix the ingredients together. Cover and cook for 5 to 10 minutes until heated through and bubbling. Taste and adjust seasoning and serve immediately.

Variations:
Canned peas or broad beans can be used instead of the carrots.

From front: Mexican meatballs; Chunky beef with herb dumplings

Savoury potato cakes

Metric	Imperial
1 × 100 g packet instant mashed potato mix	1 × 4 oz packet instant mashed potato mix
450 ml boiling water	¾ pint boiling water
4 × 15 ml spoons sage and onion stuffing mix	4 tablespoons sage and onion stuffing mix
approximately 100 g Cheddar cheese, grated	approximately 4 oz Cheddar cheese, grated
1 egg, beaten	1 egg, beaten
freshly ground black pepper	freshly ground black pepper
flour for coating	flour for coating
vegetable oil for frying	vegetable oil for frying

Cooking time: 10 minutes

Put the potato mix in a bowl and gradually stir in the boiling water. Beat in the stuffing mix, cheese, egg and plenty of black pepper. Leave to stand for 15 minutes. Shape the mixture into 8 flat cakes with floured hands, then dust lightly with flour. Heat a few spoons of oil in a frying pan, add the potato cakes and fry for 5 minutes on each side until golden brown. Serve immediately.
Makes 8

Salmon suprême

Metric	Imperial
2 × 150 g packets savoury rice	2 × 5 oz packets savoury rice
1 packet Parmesan cheese sauce mix	1 packet Parmesan cheese sauce mix
300 ml milk	½ pint milk
approximately 50 g Cheddar cheese, grated	approximately 2 oz Cheddar cheese, grated
1 × 200 g can salmon, drained and flaked	1 × 7 oz can salmon, drained and flaked
1 × 200 g can tuna, drained and flaked	1 × 7 oz can tuna, drained and flaked
1 × 200 g can button mushrooms, drained	1 × 7 oz can button mushrooms, drained
freshly ground black pepper	freshly ground black pepper
grated cheese, to serve	grated cheese, to serve

Cooking time: 30 minutes

Cook the savoury rice for 20 minutes according to packet directions. Remove from the heat, cover tightly with a lid and set aside. Make the cheese sauce with the milk according to packet directions, then gently fold in the cheese, fish and mushrooms. Add plenty of black pepper and heat through for 5 minutes. Put the rice on individual plates, pour over the sauce and sprinkle with cheese, or hand the cheese separately in a bowl. Serve immediately.

Pan pizza

Metric	Imperial
1 × 150 g packet pizza base mix	1 × 5 oz packet pizza base mix
2 × 15 ml spoons vegetable oil	2 tablespoons vegetable oil
1 onion, peeled and finely chopped	1 onion, peeled and finely chopped
1 garlic clove, peeled and crushed with 1 × 2.5 ml spoon salt	1 garlic clove, peeled and crushed with ½ teaspoon salt
1 × 425 g can minced beef in rich gravy	1 × 15 oz can minced beef in rich gravy
2 × 15 ml spoons tomato purée	2 tablespoons tomato purée
1 × 2.5 ml spoon ground allspice	½ teaspoon ground allspice
freshly ground black pepper	freshly ground black pepper
3 tomatoes, finely sliced	3 tomatoes, finely sliced
freshly chopped parsley	freshly chopped parsley

Cooking time: 30–35 minutes

If you only have one burner, make the minced beef topping first and set aside while using the burner to start cooking the pizza base.

Make the pizza base according to packet directions. Roll out the dough to a circle large enough to fit inside a non-stick skillet or frypan. Brush the inside of the pan with oil, place the dough in the bottom and leave in a warm place for 10 to 15 minutes until it starts to rise. Put the pan over the lowest possible flame, cover tightly and cook for 10 minutes.

Meanwhile, heat the oil in a separate pan, add the onion and garlic and fry gently until golden. Stir in the remaining ingredients, except the tomatoes and parsley, cook for about 5 minutes until bubbling. Taste and adjust seasoning. Spoon the minced beef mixture over the pizza base, and cover with the tomato slices. Cover and continue cooking over gentle heat for a further 20 minutes. Sprinkle with parsley, cut into wedges and serve hot with a mixed salad.

Serves 3 to 4

From front: Pan pizza; Savoury potato cakes; Salmon suprême

Strawberry mousse

Metric	Imperial
1 × 400 g can strawberries	1 × 15 oz can strawberries
1 × 150 g packet strawberry jelly	1 × 5 oz packet strawberry jelly
300 ml evaporated milk, chilled	½ pint evaporated milk, chilled

Drain the strawberries, measure the juice and make up to 450 ml/¾ pint with water. Heat 150 ml/¼ pint of the liquid to boiling point, pour it over the jelly and stir to dissolve. Stir in the remaining liquid, then chill until just beginning to set. Fold in the strawberries. Whip the evaporated milk until thick, fold it into the jelly and fruit, leaving a marbled effect if liked. Transfer to individual glasses and chill until firm.

Variations:
Any kind of canned fruit or jelly can be used instead of strawberries.
If fresh cream is available, then use this instead of the evaporated milk.

Chestnut mousse

Metric	Imperial
1 × 100 g packet melt-in-the-bag plain chocolate cake covering	1 × 4 oz packet melt-in-the-bag plain chocolate cake covering
1 × 225 g sweetened chestnut purée	1 × 8 oz can sweetened chestnut purée
2 × 15 ml spoons milk	2 tablespoons milk
150 ml double or whipping cream, stiffly whipped	¼ pint double or whipping cream, stiffly whipped
1 chocolate flake, crumbled, to decorate	1 chocolate flake, crumbled, to decorate

If you happen to have some brandy or sherry, the flavour of this mousse will benefit from a spoonful or two.

Melt the chocolate in the bag according to packet directions. Meanwhile, beat the chestnut purée in a bowl. Stir in the melted chocolate and milk and fold in the whipped cream. Spoon into a serving dish and sprinkle over the chocolate flake.

Quick gooseberry fool

Metric	Imperial
1 × 400 g can gooseberries drained	1 × 14 oz can gooseberries drained
1 × 425 g can custard	1 × 15 oz can custard
1–2 drops almond essence	1–2 drops almond essence
1 × 175 g can dairy cream, chilled	1 × 6 oz can dairy cream, chilled
2–3 × 15 ml spoons flaked blanched almonds, to decorate	2–3 tablespoons flaked blanched almonds, to decorate

Mash the gooseberries with a potato masher. Put in a bowl with the custard and almond essence and stir well to mix. Fold in the cream, then spoon into individual glasses and decorate each one with a sprinkling of flaked almonds.

Variation:
Any canned fruit can be substituted for the gooseberries.

Camper's crumble

Metric	Imperial
2 × 400 g cans apple and raspberry pie filling	2 × 14 oz cans apple and raspberry pie filling
1 × 225 g packet crumble mix	1 × 8 oz packet crumble mix
vanilla ice cream, to serve	vanilla ice cream, to serve

Cooking time: about 20 minutes

Put the pie filling in a shallow cake tin and heat until bubbling. Sprinkle over the crumble mix, cover and cook over gentle heat for 10 minutes. Transfer to a very low grill and grill for about 5 minutes until an even golden brown, turning the tin as necessary. Serve with vanilla ice cream.

Variation:
Fresh fruit can be used instead of pie filling for this crumble, but make sure it is thoroughly cooked before adding the topping.

Chestnut mousse; Strawberry mousse; Quick fool; Camper's crumble

Chocolate crunch flan

Metric	Imperial
1 × 200 g packet ginger nuts	1 × 7 oz packet ginger nuts
approximately 75 g butter or margarine, melted	approximately 3 oz butter or margarine, melted
1 × 65 g packet chocolate flavoured Angel Delight	1 × 2½ oz packet chocolate flavoured Angel Delight
150 ml milk	¼ pint milk
2 bananas	2 bananas
150 ml double cream, stiffly whipped	¼ pint double cream, stiffly whipped
1 chocolate milk flake	1 chocolate milk flake

This dessert is well worth the extra time and trouble it takes, as it will last a family of four for two days.

Put the biscuits in a bowl, crush with the end of a rolling pin, and stir in the melted butter. Press into the base and sides of a 20 cm/8 inch flan dish or shallow cake tin, then chill until firm. Beat the Angel Delight with the milk according to packet directions, spread in the bottom of the flan. Peel the bananas and slice finely, arrange them on top. Spread the cream over the bananas, then crumble over the chocolate.
Serves 6 to 8

Peach condé

Metric	Imperial
1 × 2.5 ml spoon ground cinnamon	½ teaspoon ground cinnamon
1 × 425 g can creamed rice	1 × 15 oz can creamed rice
1 × 400 g can peach halves, drained	1 × 14 oz can peach halves, drained
4 glacé cherries, halved, to finish	4 glacé cherries, halved, to finish

Stir the cinnamon into the rice. Chop the peaches finely, reserving 4 halves for decoration. Layer the rice and peaches in 4 individual glasses, starting and ending with a layer of rice. Top with the reserved peach halves and decorate with halved glacé cherries. Chill before serving.

Variation:
You can vary the fruit, according to taste and availability.

Peach condé; Chocolate crunch flan

Black Forest cherry cake; Lemon snow

Black Forest cherry cake

Metric
1 × 425 g can black
  cherries
1 × 5 ml spoon arrowroot
1 chocolate-flavoured
  sponge sandwich
150 ml double cream,
  stiffly whipped
1 chocolate milk flake

Imperial
1 × 15 oz can black
  cherries
1 teaspoon arrowroot
1 chocolate-flavoured
  sponge sandwich
¼ pint double cream,
  stiffly whipped
1 chocolate milk flake

You can serve this either as a pudding, or a rich cake at tea-time.

Drain and pit the cherries, reserving the juice. Mix the arrowroot with a little of the juice in a pan, then stir in the remaining juice and bring slowly to the boil. Simmer for a few minutes until the sauce thickens, stirring constantly. Remove from the heat, pour into a jug and leave to cool.
Separate the two layers of the cake and cut the top layer into serving portions. Fold the cherries into the cream, then spread over the bottom layer of the cake. Place the portions of cake on top at an angle, then crumble over the chocolate.
Serve the sauce separately.

Lemon snow

Metric
1 × 50 g packet lemon
  pie filling
300 ml water
2 eggs, separated
4 × 15 ml spoons sugar
1 × 25 g packet Dream
  Topping
multi-coloured sugar
  strands, to decorate

Imperial
1 × 2 oz packet lemon
  pie filling
½ pint water
2 eggs, separated
4 tablespoons sugar
1 × 1 oz packet Dream
  Topping
multi-coloured sugar
  strands, to decorate

This is a dessert which the children will love.

Make the lemon pie filling according to packet directions with the water and 2 egg yolks. Leave to cool.
Beat the egg whites until stiff, add the sugar and beat again until shiny. Make the Dream Topping according to packet directions, then fold half into the lemon mixture with the egg whites. Transfer to individual glasses and spread the remaining Dream Topping over the top. Sprinkle with sugar strands and chill until firm.

ONE-BURNER MEALS

If you are travelling light and your only cooking facility is a one-burner camping stove, then you will have to exercise a little ingenuity when it comes to meal times. In the first place, you will need to invest in a set of stacking pans – these will make it possible for you to heat through vegetables or rice on top of your main dish so that you are not always limited to eating bread or salad with every meal.

An alternative way to make sure you have vegetables with your meals is to incorporate them into the main dish, and as long as you take with you a large enough pan you should always be able to do this.

Cheese and bacon frizzles

Metric	Imperial
1 large potato, peeled and grated	1 large potato, peeled and grated
½ onion, peeled and very finely chopped	½ onion, peeled and very finely chopped
50 g Cheddar or Edam cheese, grated	2 oz Cheddar or Edam cheese, grated
4 rashers back bacon, de-rinded and finely chopped	4 rashers back bacon, de-rinded and finely chopped
4 × 15 ml spoons self-raising flour	4 tablespoons self-raising flour
1 egg, beaten	1 egg, beaten
freshly ground black pepper	freshly ground black pepper
4 × 15 ml spoons vegetable oil	4 tablespoons vegetable oil

Cooking time: 15 minutes

If your frying pan is not large enough to hold this amount of mixture all at once, then you will have to cook the frizzles in two batches.

Put all the ingredients in a bowl, except the oil, and beat well. Heat the oil in a large non-stick frying pan. Add the mixture to the pan in spoonfuls and fry for 7 minutes on each side until golden brown and crisp. Serve immediately with a tossed mixed salad or baked beans.
Makes 8

Minestrone medley

Metric	Imperial
2 × 15 ml spoons vegetable oil	2 tablespoons vegetable oil
1 onion, peeled and finely chopped	1 onion, peeled and finely chopped
175 g piece garlic sausage, cut into thin strips	6 oz piece garlic sausage, cut into thin strips
1 × 400 g can tomatoes	1 × 14 oz can tomatoes
2 handfuls (94 ml) macaroni	2 handfuls (⅓ cup) macaroni
600 ml water	1 pint water
1 × 25 g packet quick dried garden peas	1 × 1 oz packet quick dried garden peas
1 × 2.5 ml spoon dried oregano	½ teaspoon dried oregano
freshly ground black pepper	freshly ground black pepper
1 × 425 g can red kidney beans, drained	1 × 15 oz can red kidney beans, drained
1 × 425 g can cut green beans, drained	1 × 15 oz can cut green beans, drained
grated Parmesan cheese, to serve	grated Parmesan cheese, to serve

Cooking time: 30 minutes

Heat the oil in a large saucepan, add the onion and fry over gentle heat until soft. Add the garlic sausage and fry for 5 minutes, then add the remaining ingredients except the beans and cheese. Stir well to mix. Bring to the boil, cover and simmer over gentle heat for 15 minutes, stirring occasionally. Stir in the beans and simmer for a further 5 minutes or until the pasta is tender. Taste and adjust seasoning, adding plenty of black pepper. Serve hot with the Parmesan handed separately.

Variations:
Any kind of cooked or canned meat can be substituted for the garlic sausage – corned beef, pork shoulder, ham sausage, chopped ham loaf, etc.
Quick dried mixed vegetables or a small can of broad beans can be used instead of the peas and green beans, and other egg noodles used for the macaroni.

Cheese and bacon frizzles; Minestrone medley

Tagliatelle bolognese

Metric	Imperial
2 × 15 ml spoons vegetable oil	2 tablespoons vegetable oil
1 onion, peeled and finely chopped	1 onion, peeled and finely chopped
1 garlic clove, peeled and crushed	1 garlic clove, peeled and crushed
750 g minced beef	1½ lb minced beef
1 × 275 can condensed cream of tomato soup	1 × 10 oz can condensed cream of tomato soup
300 ml water	½ pint water
1 × 225 g can tomatoes	1 × 8 oz can tomatoes
1 × 5 ml spoon dried oregano	1 teaspoon dried oregano
salt	salt
freshly ground black pepper	freshly ground black pepper
225 g (900 ml) tagliatelle noodles	8 oz (1½ pint) tagliatelle noodles
grated Parmesan cheese, to serve	grated Parmesan cheese, to serve

Cooking time: 30–35 minutes

Heat the oil in a pan, add the onion and garlic and fry over gentle heat until soft. Add the meat and fry until browned, breaking it up constantly with a spoon. Stir in the remaining ingredients except the noodles and bring to the boil. Simmer for 20 minutes, stirring occasionally, then add the noodles. Cover and simmer for a further 10 minutes or until the noodles are soft, adding a little water if the mixture becomes dry. Taste and adjust seasoning, then serve immediately with Parmesan cheese handed separately.

Liver stroganoff; Pigs in blankets; Tagliatelle bolognese

Pigs in blankets

Metric	Imperial
4 rashers streaky bacon, de-rinded	4 rashers streaky bacon, de-rinded
prepared French mustard	prepared French mustard
4 frankfurters	4 frankfurters
2 × 15 ml spoons vegetable oil	2 tablespoons vegetable oil
4 long soft rolls	4 long soft rolls
butter for spreading	butter for spreading
75–100 g coleslaw	3–4 oz coleslaw

Cooking time: 10 minutes

Spread one side of the bacon rashers with a little mustard. Wrap a bacon rasher around each frankfurter, with the mustard on the inside. Heat the oil in a frying pan. Add the frankfurters and fry for 10 minutes over brisk heat, shaking the pan occasionally until the bacon is browned on all sides.

Meanwhile, split the rolls in half lengthways and spread the cut surfaces with butter and a little mustard, if liked. Place one frankfurter in each roll, then top with coleslaw.

Makes 4

Variations:
Skinless sausages can be substituted for the frankfurters, although they will need to be cooked an extra 5 minutes.

Any kind of salad can be used instead of coleslaw, or the rolls can be filled with tomato and cucumber slices and lettuce, then dressed with mayonnaise.

Liver stroganoff

Metric	Imperial
1 large knob of butter	*1 large knob of butter*
1 onion, peeled and finely chopped	*1 onion, peeled and finely chopped*
500 g lamb's liver, sliced into very thin strips	*1 lb lamb's liver, sliced into very thin strips*
1 × 15 ml spoon tomato purée	*1 tablespoon tomato purée*
1 × 15 ml spoon Worcestershire sauce	*1 tablespoon Worcestershire sauce*
juice of 1 lemon	*juice of 1 lemon*
225 g button mushrooms, finely sliced	*½ lb button mushrooms, finely sliced*
salt	*salt*
freshly ground black pepper	*freshly ground black pepper*
150 ml soured cream	*¼ pint soured cream*

Cooking time: 15 minutes

Melt the butter in a pan, add the onion and fry over gentle heat until soft. Add the liver and fry for 5 minutes, stirring constantly. Stir in the remaining ingredients except the cream, then cook for a further 5 minutes, stirring occasionally. Remove from the heat and stir in the cream, return the pan to a low heat and warm through. Taste and adjust seasoning and serve with a tossed green salad and boiled rice.

Chicken tetrazzini

Metric	Imperial
1 large knob of butter	1 large knob of butter
1 onion, peeled and finely chopped	1 onion, peeled and finely chopped
4 chicken portions, skinned	4 chicken portions, skinned
2 × 15 ml spoons flour	2 tablespoons flour
1 × 400 g can tomatoes	1 × 14 oz can tomatoes
450 ml water	¾ pint water
1 chicken stock cube	1 chicken stock cube
4 medium carrots, peeled and very finely sliced	4 medium carrots, peeled and very finely sliced
1 × 2.5 ml spoon dried tarragon	½ teaspoon dried tarragon
salt	salt
freshly ground black pepper	freshly ground black pepper
300 ml finely broken spaghetti	½ pint finely broken spaghetti
175 g mushrooms, sliced	6 oz mushrooms, sliced
grated Parmesan cheese, to serve	grated Parmesan cheese, to serve

Cooking time: 60 minutes

Melt the butter in a large saucepan, add the onion and fry over gentle heat until soft. Add the chicken, sprinkle over the flour, then fry until browned on both sides. Stir in the tomatoes and water. Bring to the boil, stirring constantly, add the stock cube and stir to dissolve. Add the carrots, tarragon and salt and pepper to taste, then cover and simmer for 25 minutes, stirring occasionally. Add the spaghetti and simmer for a further 15 minutes, then add the mushrooms. Stir well to mix, simmer for a further 5 minutes or until the chicken is cooked and the spaghetti is tender.

Taste and adjust seasoning. Serve immediately with a tossed green salad and the Parmesan handed separately.

Risotto

Metric	Imperial
1 large knob of butter	1 large knob of butter
1 large onion, peeled and chopped	1 large onion, peeled and chopped
2 × 150 g packets savoury tomato rice	2 × 5 oz packets savoury tomato rice
900 ml hot water	1½ pints hot water
1 × 50 g packet quick dried mixed vegetables	1 × 2 oz packet quick dried mixed vegetables
freshly ground black pepper	freshly ground black pepper
100 g piece of garlic sausage, diced	4 oz piece of garlic sausage, diced
6 small frankfurters, sliced	6 small frankfurters, sliced
grated Parmesan cheese, to serve	grated Parmesan cheese, to serve

Cooking time: 35 minutes

Melt the butter in a large saucepan, add the onion and fry over gentle heat until soft. Stir in the rice and fry for a further 5 minutes, stirring occasionally. Pour in the water, stir once, then bring to the boil. Add the mixed vegetables and pepper to taste, cover tightly and cook over gentle heat for 20 minutes until most of the liquid has been absorbed. Stir in the garlic sausage and frankfurters and cook for a further 5 minutes until heated through. Taste and adjust seasoning, then serve immediately with a tossed mixed salad and the Parmesan handed separately.

Variation:
As an alternative to the garlic sausage and frankfurters used here, you can use diced cooked chicken and fresh prawns or mussels, if available.

Tortilla

Metric	Imperial
2 × 15 ml spoons vegetable oil	2 tablespoons vegetable oil
1 large onion, peeled and finely sliced	1 large onion, peeled and finely sliced
2 garlic cloves, peeled and crushed	2 garlic cloves, peeled and crushed
4 medium potatoes, peeled and cut into small dice	4 medium potatoes, peeled and cut into small dice
6 eggs, beaten	6 eggs, beaten
salt	salt
freshly ground black pepper	freshly ground black pepper
1 × 200 g can sweetcure ham, cut into small dice	1 × 7 oz can sweetcure ham, cut into small dice

Cooking time: 35 minutes

Heat the oil in a large skillet or frypan, add the onion and fry over gentle heat until soft. Add the garlic and potatoes, cover and cook over gentle heat for 20 minutes or until the potatoes are tender. Increase the heat, pour in the eggs and season with salt and pepper to taste. Cook over high heat for 5 minutes, stirring with a fork and shaking the pan to allow the uncooked egg to set. Add the ham, lower the heat, cover and cook for a further 5 minutes or until the omelette is set on top. Serve immediately with a tossed mixed salad.

Variations:
Try making the omelette with canned mushrooms, peas, prawns or sweetcorn instead of the ham, or simply stir in any leftover meat or vegetables.

From rear: Risotto; Chicken tetrazzini; Tortilla

37

Spicy ham fritters

Fish chowder

Metric	Imperial
1 large knob of butter	1 large knob of butter
1 onion, peeled and finely chopped	1 onion, peeled and finely chopped
3 celery sticks, chopped	3 celery sticks, chopped
3 bacon rashers, de-rinded and chopped	3 bacon rashers, de-rinded and chopped
2 × 15 ml spoons flour	2 tablespoons flour
900 ml milk and water, mixed	1½ pints milk and water, mixed
3 medium potatoes, peeled and diced	3 medium potatoes, peeled and diced
pinch of dried mixed herbs	pinch of dried mixed herbs
pinch of ground turmeric	pinch of ground turmeric
salt	salt
freshly ground black pepper	freshly ground black pepper
225 g white fish fillets, skinned and cut into pieces	8 oz white fish fillets, skinned and cut into pieces
1 × 200 g can tuna, drained and flaked	1 × 7 oz can tuna, drained and flaked

Cooking time: 30–35 minutes

Make this fish stew with freshly caught fish if you are staying near the sea.

Melt the butter in a pan, add the onion, celery and bacon and fry over gentle heat for 5 minutes, stirring occasionally. Stir in the flour and cook for 1 minute. Gradually stir in the milk and water. Bring to the boil, add the potatoes, herbs, turmeric and salt and pepper to taste.
Cover and simmer for 10 minutes, add the white fish and simmer for a further 10 minutes. Add the tuna and heat through for 5 minutes, then taste and adjust seasoning. Serve hot with crusty rolls and butter.

Variations:
Any kind of fish can be used – fresh cod, haddock or whiting go well with tuna, or use prawns or mussels if available.

Prawn savoury

Metric	Imperial
2 × 15 ml spoons vegetable oil	2 tablespoons vegetable oil
1 onion, peeled and finely chopped	1 onion, peeled and finely chopped
4 tomatoes, quartered	4 tomatoes, quartered
1 × 1.25 ml spoon ground turmeric	¼ teaspoon ground turmeric
1 coffee mug (300 ml) long-grain rice	1 coffee mug (½ pint) long-grain rice
1½ coffee mugs (450 ml) water	1½ coffee mugs (¾ pint) water
1 chicken stock cube	1 chicken stock cube
freshly ground black pepper	freshly ground black pepper
225 g peeled prawns	8 oz peeled prawns
1 green or red pepper, cored, seeded and finely chopped	1 green or red pepper, cored, seeded and finely chopped

Cooking time: 30 minutes

Heat the oil in a pan, add the onion, tomatoes and turmeric and fry over gentle heat for 10 minutes until soft, stirring occasionally. Add the rice and water, stir once and bring to the boil. Add the stock cube and stir until dissolved, then add plenty of pepper. Lower the heat, cover with a tight fitting lid and cook gently for 20 minutes until the rice is 'al dente'. Stir in the prawns 5 minutes before the end of cooking, taste and adjust seasoning. Sprinkle with the pepper. Serve hot with a cucumber or tomato salad and crusty French bread and butter.

Variations:
Substitute 4 chopped frankfurters for the prawns, or 1 × 200 g/7 oz can tuna fish, flaked.
Serves 2 to 3

Spicy ham fritters

Metric
1 × 100 g packet pancake
   and batter mix
about 200 ml milk
1 × 350 g can chopped
   ham loaf
curry paste
vegetable oil for shallow
   frying

Imperial
1 × 4 oz packet pancake
   and batter mix
about ⅓ pint milk
1 × 12 oz can chopped
   ham loaf
curry paste
vegetable oil for shallow
   frying

Cooking time: 10 minutes

Make up a coating batter with the mix and the milk according to packet directions. Cut the ham loaf into 8 equal slices, spread one side of each slice with a little curry paste. Heat the oil in a non-stick frying pan. Dip the ham slices into the batter one at a time until evenly coated. Fry in the hot oil for 5 minutes on each side until golden brown and crisp, then drain on paper towels. Serve immediately with a tomato salad and crisp French bread and butter.

Variations:
Substitute creamed horseradish, prepared mustard, garlic pepper or yeast extract for the curry paste.

Fish chowder; Prawn savoury

Chilli con carne

Metric	Imperial
2 × 15 ml spoons vegetable oil	2 tablespoons vegetable oil
2 onions, peeled and finely chopped	2 onions, peeled and finely chopped
1 garlic clove, peeled and crushed	1 garlic clove, peeled and crushed
750 g minced beef	1½ lb minced beef
1 × 5 ml spoon chilli powder, or to taste	1 teaspoon chilli powder, or to taste
1 × 400 g can tomatoes	1 × 14 oz can tomatoes
3 × 15 ml spoons tomato purée	3 tablespoons tomato purée
1 × 5 ml spoon sugar	1 teaspoon sugar
salt	salt
freshly ground black pepper	freshly ground black pepper
1 × 425 g can red kidney beans, drained	1 × 15 oz can red kidney beans, drained

Cooking time: 30 minutes

Chilli powder is very hot and varies in strength according to the brand used, so use it cautiously.

Heat the oil in a pan, add the onion and garlic and fry over gentle heat until soft, stirring occasionally. Add the beef and fry until browned, breaking the meat up with a spoon. Add the remaining ingredients except the beans, and stir well to mix. Bring to the boil, lower the heat and cook gently for 20 minutes. Add the beans and heat through for 5 minutes, then taste and adjust seasoning. Serve hot with yogurt, boiled rice and a tossed green salad.

40

Curried eggs; Chilli con carne; Pork and pepper casserole

Pork and pepper casserole

Metric	Imperial
2 × 15 ml spoons vegetable oil	2 tablespoons vegetable oil
1 onion, peeled and finely chopped	1 onion, peeled and finely chopped
750 g pork fillet, cut into small cubes	1½ lb pork fillet, cut into small cubes
1½ × 15 ml spoons flour	1½ tablespoons flour
2 × 15 ml spoons soy sauce	2 tablespoons soy sauce
few drops of Tabasco sauce	few drops of Tabasco sauce
6 × 15 ml spoons undiluted orange squash	6 tablespoons undiluted orange squash
300 ml water	½ pint water
1 chicken stock cube	1 chicken stock cube
freshly ground black pepper	freshly ground black pepper
2 red or green peppers, cored, seeded and cut into rings	2 red or green peppers, cored, seeded and cut into rings
100 g Chinese egg noodles, broken into pieces	4 oz Chinese egg noodles, broken into pieces

Cooking time: 1 hour 10 minutes

Heat the oil in a pan, add the onion and fry over gentle heat until soft. Coat the pork in the flour, then fry until browned on all sides. Stir in the soy and Tabasco sauces, orange squash and water. Bring to the boil, add the stock cube and stir to dissolve. Add pepper to taste, cover and simmer for 1 hour or until the pork is tender. Add the peppers and noodles 10 minutes before the end of cooking, stirring occasionally to separate the noodles. Taste and adjust seasoning. Serve hot with French bread and salad.

Curried eggs

Metric	Imperial
2 × 15 ml spoons vegetable oil	2 tablespoons vegetable oil
1 onion, peeled and finely chopped	1 onion, peeled and finely chopped
1 eating apple, peeled, cored and chopped	1 eating apple, peeled, cored and chopped
2 × 15 ml spoons curry paste	2 tablespoons curry paste
1 × 15 ml spoon flour	1 tablespoon flour
300 ml water	½ pint water
1 chicken stock cube	1 chicken stock cube
1 × 15 ml spoon tomato purée	1 tablespoon tomato purée
4 hard-boiled eggs, halved	4 hard-boiled eggs, halved
1 × 350 g can pre-cooked pilau (savoury fried) rice	1 × 12 oz can pre-cooked pilau (savoury fried) rice
salt	salt
freshly ground black pepper	freshly ground black pepper

Cooking time: about 30 minutes

Heat the oil in a pan, add the onion and apple and fry over gentle heat until golden. Stir in the curry paste and fry for 5 minutes, stirring constantly. Stir in the flour and fry for a further minute, then stir in the water gradually. Bring to the boil, add the stock cube and tomato purée and stir well to dissolve the stock cube. Lower the heat and cook gently for 5 minutes, then add the eggs, cut side uppermost. Spoon the sauce over the yolks, cover with a lid and set aside. Put the pilau rice in a separate stacking pan. Add a little water and heat through for 3 minutes according to directions on the can. Break up the rice with a fork while cooking. Stack the pan of rice on top of the pan of eggs and place on the burner. Cover and cook over the lowest possible heat for 10 minutes. Taste and adjust the seasoning of the sauce, serve with mango chutney and a side salad of yogurt and cucumber.
Serves 2

Corned beef hash

Metric
1 × 100 g packet instant
　mashed potato mix
450 ml boiling water
2 large knobs of butter
1 × 1.25 ml spoon
　mustard powder
freshly ground black pepper
1 × 350 g can corned beef,
　shredded
1 onion, peeled and
　finely chopped

Imperial
1 × 4 oz packet instant
　mashed potato mix
¾ pint boiling water
2 large knobs of butter
¼ teaspoon
　mustard powder
freshly ground black pepper
1 × 12 oz can corned beef,
　shredded
1 onion, peeled and
　finely chopped

Cooking time: about 25 minutes

Put the potato mix in a bowl, then gradually stir in the boiling water. Add half the butter, the mustard and plenty of pepper and beat well to mix. Fold in the corned beef.

Melt the remaining butter in a non-stick frying pan, add the onion and fry over gentle heat until soft. Add the potato mixture and fry over brisk heat for 10 minutes. Stir the mixture and turn it over occasionally, flatten it into a cake shape with a spatula and smooth the top. Fry over moderate heat for 5 minutes or until golden brown underneath. Invert a plate over the pan and turn the hash out onto the plate. Slide back into the pan and fry for a further 5 minutes or until golden brown on the underside. Cut into wedges and serve hot with baked beans.

To serve both the hash and baked beans hot at the same time: cover the hash with a tight fitting lid as soon as it is cooked, then remove from the heat. Cook the beans quickly over brisk heat while cutting the hash into wedges.

Spanish beef

Metric
2 × 15 ml spoons vegetable
　oil
1 onion, peeled and
　finely chopped
1 garlic clove, peeled
　and crushed
2 green or red peppers,
　cored, seeded and
　finely chopped
2 × 425 g cans chunky
　steak in rich gravy
2 × 15 ml spoons tomato
　purée
1 × 2.5 ml spoon dried
　tarragon
pinch of sugar
salt
freshly ground black pepper
50 g stuffed olives

Imperial
2 tablespoons vegetable
　oil
1 onion, peeled and
　finely chopped
1 garlic clove, peeled
　and crushed
2 green or red peppers,
　cored, seeded and
　finely chopped
2 × 15 oz cans chunky
　steak in rich gravy
2 tablespoons tomato
　purée
½ teaspoon dried
　tarragon
pinch of sugar
salt
freshly ground black pepper
2 oz stuffed olives

Cooking time: 25 minutes

If you happen to have a bottle of red wine open, then add a few spoonfuls to this dish to give body and flavour.

Heat the oil in a pan, add the onion, garlic and peppers and fry over gentle heat for 10 minutes, stirring occasionally. Add the remaining ingredients, except the olives, and cook over gentle heat for 10 minutes until bubbling. Add the olives and heat through for 5 minutes. Taste and adjust seasoning.

Serve with instant mashed potato, pre-cooked rice or crusty French bread and butter.

Spanish beef; Corned beef hash

Sponge in the pan

Metric	Imperial
1 × 400 g can peach halves	1 × 14 oz can peach halves
4 × 15 ml spoons soft brown sugar	4 tablespoons soft brown sugar
1 large knob of butter	1 large knob of butter
1 × 2.5 ml spoon ground cinnamon	½ teaspoon ground cinnamon
1 × 150 g packet sponge mix	1 × 5 oz packet sponge mix
1 egg	1 egg
2 × 15 ml spoons sugar	2 tablespoons sugar
2 × 15 ml spoons milk	2 tablespoons milk

Cooking time: 30–35 minutes

Drain the peaches and pour the juice into a 18–20 cm/ 7–8 inch non-stick saucepan. Add the brown sugar, butter and cinnamon and bring to the boil, stirring constantly. Lower the heat and simmer until dark and thick. Meanwhile, make the sponge mix according to packet directions with the egg, sugar and milk.

Arrange the peaches cut sides uppermost in the saucepan. Spoon over the sponge batter evenly and smooth the top. Cover and cook over low heat for 30 minutes or until the sponge is set. Leave to stand for 10 minutes, then invert a plate over the pan, and turn the sponge out on to the plate, peach side uppermost. Serve with fresh cream or vanilla ice cream.

Serves 5 to 6

Variations:
Any kind of canned fruit can be used instead of the peaches.

Dried fruit compôte

Metric	Imperial
2 × 225 g packets mixed dried fruit (apples, apricots, prunes, figs, etc), soaked overnight in cold water	2 × 8 oz packets mixed dried fruit (apples, apricots, prunes, figs, etc), soaked overnight in cold water
6 × 15 ml spoons undiluted orange squash	6 tablespoons undiluted orange squash
1 × 2.5 ml spoon ground cinnamon	½ teaspoon ground cinnamon
4 × 15 ml spoons brown sugar	4 tablespoons brown sugar
flaked almonds or chopped mixed nuts, to finish	flaked almonds or chopped mixed nuts, to finish

Cooking time: 20–25 minutes

Serve this as a dessert with fresh cream or ice cream. It is also good at breakfast time with homemade muesli or other cereals, and yogurt.

Drain the dried fruits, then put in a pan with the orange squash, cinnamon and sugar. Add enough water to just cover and stir well to mix. Bring to the boil and simmer for 15 to 20 minutes or until soft. Leave to cool, then chill. Sprinkle with nuts before serving.

Keeps for up to one week

Right: Dried fruit compôte; Glazed bananas
Below: Sponge in the pan

Glazed bananas

Metric	Imperial
1 large knob of butter	*1 large knob of butter*
3 × 15 ml spoons soft brown sugar	*3 tablespoons soft brown sugar*
3 × 15 ml spoons undiluted orange squash	*3 tablespoons undiluted orange squash*
1 × 15 ml spoon golden syrup	*1 tablespoon golden syrup*
1 × 1.25 ml spoon ground cinnamon	*¼ teaspoon ground cinnamon*
2 bananas, peeled and split in half lengthways	*2 bananas, peeled and split in half lengthways*

Cooking time: 10 minutes

Melt the butter in a non-stick frying pan. Add the sugar, orange squash, syrup and cinnamon and heat gently until melted, stirring constantly. Add the bananas and cook over gentle heat for 10 minutes until soft and glazed, spooning the sauce over them during the cooking. Serve hot with chilled cream or ice cream.
Serves 2

TWO BURNERS PLUS GRILL

Cooking on a two burner plus grill need not be very different from cooking at home. Although you are having to cope with two burners less than usual, holiday meals are rarely as involved as those cooked at home. If you plan your meals in advance and prepare as many of the ingredients as you can beforehand, then you should be able to deal with the limited space and facilities. It is also essential to work out which saucepans are to be used for what, and a set of stacking pans will make life easier.

Utilize every inch of pan space to avoid a lot of washing up: a triple pan set which combines three saucepans in one is a useful investment, and remember also to use saucepans for mixing and beating rather than separate bowls. Although the burners on this type of stove are very similar to those on a domestic cooker, the grill does need rather more attention. Be careful not to use deep pans or dishes under the grill, or the food can easily burn. It is best to use the grill pan provided if possible. Always preheat the grill for about 5 minutes before use, and keep an eye on the food while grilling so that you can turn it round should it begin to brown unevenly.

Spicy beef cakes in tomato sauce

Metric	Imperial
2 slices of bread, crusts removed, broken into pieces	2 slices of bread, crusts removed, broken into pieces
500 g minced beef	1 lb minced beef
1 onion, peeled and very finely chopped	1 onion, peeled and very finely chopped
1 × 15 ml spoon tomato purée	1 tablespoon tomato purée
1 × 15 ml spoon Worcestershire sauce	1 tablespoon Worcestershire sauce
salt	salt
freshly ground black pepper	freshly ground black pepper
flour for coating	flour for coating
2 × 15 ml spoons vegetable oil	2 tablespoons vegetable oil
1 × 225 g can tomato sauce	1 × 8 oz can tomato sauce
1 × 2.5 ml spoon dried oregano or basil	½ teaspoon dried oregano or basil
soured cream or plain unsweetened yogurt, to finish	soured cream or plain unsweetened yogurt, to finish

Cooking time: 35 minutes

Put the bread in a small bowl and cover with water. Leave to stand for 10 minutes, then squeeze dry. Mix the bread with the beef, onion, tomato purée, Worcestershire sauce and salt and pepper to taste. Form the mixture into 8 flat cakes, then coat in flour. Heat the oil in a frying pan, add the beef cakes and fry over brisk heat for 5 minutes on each side. Lower the heat and pour over the sauce. Sprinkle each cake with a little oregano or basil. Cover and cook gently for 25 minutes, then spoon over the soured cream or yogurt. Serve hot on a bed of boiled rice.

Spicy beef cakes in tomato sauce

Ham and egg supper

Metric	Imperial
1 kg new potatoes, scrubbed and halved	*2 lb new potatoes, scrubbed and halved*
salt	*salt*
2 large knobs of butter	*2 large knobs of butter*
1 onion, peeled and finely sliced	*1 onion, peeled and finely sliced*
2 green or red peppers, cored, seeded and finely sliced	*2 green or red peppers, cored, seeded and finely sliced*
1 × 500 g can cooked ham, cut into thin strips	*1 × 1 lb can cooked ham, cut into thin strips*
2 × 15 ml spoons vegetable oil	*2 tablespoons vegetable oil*
4 eggs	*4 eggs*
freshly ground black pepper	*freshly ground black pepper*

Cooking time: 35 minutes

Put the potatoes in a pan of boiling salted water, bring back to the boil, cover and simmer for 10 minutes. Drain, leave to cool slightly and slice thickly. Melt the butter in a large frying pan, add the onion and peppers and fry over gentle heat until soft. Add the potatoes and fry for about 15 minutes until golden brown, turning often during cooking.
Add the ham and fold into the potato mixture until evenly mixed. Add salt and pepper to taste, heat through for 5 minutes. Meanwhile, fry the eggs in the oil in a separate pan. Arrange the eggs on top of the potato mixture and serve immediately.

Curried meatballs

Metric	Imperial
2 slices of bread, crusts removed, broken into pieces	*2 slices of bread, crusts removed, broken into pieces*
500 g minced beef	*1 lb minced beef*
1 × 15 ml spoon curry paste	*1 tablespoon curry paste*
1 × 15 ml spoon tomato purée	*1 tablespoon tomato purée*
salt	*salt*
freshly ground black pepper	*freshly ground black pepper*
flour for coating	*flour for coating*
4 × 15 ml spoons oil	*4 tablespoons oil*
1 onion, peeled and finely chopped	*1 onion, peeled and finely chopped*
4 tomatoes, chopped	*4 tomatoes, chopped*
1 × 275 g can curry sauce	*1 × 10 oz can curry sauce*
150 ml water	*¼ pint water*

Cooking time: 40 minutes

Put the bread in a small bowl and cover with water. Leave to stand for 10 minutes, then squeeze dry. Mix the bread with the beef, curry paste, tomato purée and salt and pepper. Form the mixture into about 20 balls and coat in flour.
Heat 3 × 15 ml spoons/3 tablespoons oil in a frying pan, add the meatballs a few at a time and fry until browned on all sides. Remove from the pan with a slotted spoon and drain. Heat the remaining oil in a large saucepan, add the onion and tomatoes and fry over gentle heat for 5 minutes, stirring occasionally. Add the curry sauce and water and bring to the boil. Lower the heat, add the meatballs, cover and simmer for 25 minutes. Serve with boiled rice.

Chicken and cheese grill

Metric	Imperial
4 chicken portions, skinned	*4 chicken portions, skinned*
2 garlic cloves, peeled	*2 garlic cloves, peeled*
and slivered	*and slivered*
2 large knobs of butter	*2 large knobs of butter*
150 ml water	*¼ pint water*
salt	*salt*
freshly ground black pepper	*freshly ground black pepper*
1 × 300 ml packet cheese	*1 × ½ pint packet cheese*
sauce mix	*sauce mix*
300 ml milk	*½ pint milk*
75 g Cheddar cheese	*3 oz Cheddar cheese*
2 small packets plain	*2 small packets plain*
crisps, crushed	*crisps, crushed*

Cooking time: 1 hour

Make several incisions in the chicken flesh with a sharp knife and insert the slivers of garlic. Melt the butter in a large frying pan, add the chicken and fry until golden brown on both sides. Add the water and sprinkle with salt and pepper to taste. Cover with foil and simmer for 40 minutes until the liquid is absorbed, turning the portions once during cooking. Meanwhile, make the cheese sauce with the milk according to packet directions. Pour over the chicken and grate the cheese over the top. Sprinkle with the crisps, then put under a low grill for 10 minutes until golden brown, turning the pan occasionally to ensure even browning. Serve hot with a mixed salad or seasonal green vegetables and noodles or rice.

Chicken and cheese grill

Chicken paprikash

Metric	Imperial
1 large knob of butter	1 large knob of butter
1 onion, peeled and finely chopped	1 onion, peeled and finely chopped
1–2 × 5 ml spoons paprika pepper	1–2 teaspoons paprika pepper
1 × 15 ml spoon flour	1 tablespoon flour
4 chicken portions, skinned	4 chicken portions, skinned
4 large tomatoes, quartered	4 large tomatoes, quartered
150 ml water	¼ pint water
1 chicken stock cube	1 chicken stock cube
pinch of sugar	pinch of sugar
salt	salt
freshly ground black pepper	freshly ground black pepper
1 × 150 ml carton soured cream or plain unsweetened yogurt, to finish	1 × ¼ pint carton soured cream or plain unsweetened yogurt, to finish

Cooking time: 50 minutes

Melt the butter in a large frying pan, add the onion and paprika and fry over gentle heat for 5 minutes, stirring occasionally. Push the onions to one side. Sprinkle the flour over the chicken, add to the pan and fry until browned on both sides. Add the tomatoes and water, bring to the boil, add the stock cube and stir to dissolve. Add the sugar and salt and pepper to taste. Cover and cook over low heat for 20 minutes on each side, spooning the sauce over the chicken occasionally.

Remove the chicken from the pan, stir in the soured cream or yogurt. Heat through gently, stirring constantly. Taste and adjust seasoning and pour over the chicken. Serve with boiled rice or noodles and a seasonal green vegetable or a tossed salad.

Ratatouille

Metric	Imperial
2 small aubergines, thinly sliced	2 small aubergines, thinly sliced
salt	salt
3 × 15 ml spoons olive oil	3 tablespoons olive oil
1 onion, peeled and sliced into rings	1 onion, peeled and sliced into rings
2 garlic cloves, peeled and crushed	2 garlic cloves, peeled and crushed
1 green or red pepper, cored, seeded and sliced into rings	1 green or red pepper, cored, seeded and sliced into rings
4 small courgettes, thinly sliced	4 small courgettes, thinly sliced
4 tomatoes, quartered	4 tomatoes, quartered
freshly ground black pepper	freshly ground black pepper

Cooking time: 40 minutes

Put the aubergines on a large plate and sprinkle liberally with salt. Leave for 30 minutes. Rinse thoroughly under cold running water and drain.

Heat the oil in a large saucepan, add the onion, garlic and pepper and fry over gentle heat for 10 minutes. Add the aubergines, courgettes and tomatoes, then add plenty of salt and pepper. Cover and cook over moderate heat for 30 minutes, stirring occasionally. Taste and adjust seasoning. Serve hot as a vegetable dish. Alternatively, serve chilled as a first course or vegetable accompaniment to cold meats.

Ratatouille; Chicken paprikash

Italian pasta pot

Metric	Imperial
2 × 15 ml spoons vegetable oil	2 tablespoons vegetable oil
1 onion, peeled and finely chopped	1 onion, peeled and finely chopped
750 g minced beef	1½ lb minced beef
2 × 15 ml spoons tomato purée	2 tablespoons tomato purée
1 × 400 g can tomatoes	1 × 14 oz can tomatoes
150 ml water	¼ pint water
1 × 2.5 ml spoon dried oregano or basil	½ teaspoon dried oregano or basil
salt	salt
freshly ground black pepper	freshly ground black pepper
5 handfuls (½ pint) cut macaroni	5 handfuls (½ pint) cut macaroni
100 g Cheddar cheese	4 oz Cheddar cheese

Cooking time: 40 minutes

Heat the oil in a large shallow pan, add the onion and fry over gentle heat until soft. Add the meat and fry until browned, breaking it up constantly with a spoon. Stir in the remaining ingredients except the cheese, then bring to the boil, stirring constantly. Lower the heat and simmer for 25 minutes, then taste and adjust seasoning. Remove from the heat and grate the cheese over the top of the mixture. Put under a hot grill for 10 minutes until golden brown. Serve hot with a tossed green salad.

Variations:
Any kind of pasta can be used – broken spaghetti or tagliatelle, pasta shells, etc.

Sweet and sour chicken

Metric	Imperial
1 large knob of butter	1 large knob of butter
4 boned chicken breasts, skinned and thinly sliced	4 boned chicken breasts, skinned and thinly sliced
1 × 225 g can sliced pineapple	1 × 8 oz can sliced pineapple
1 green pepper, cored, seeded and finely chopped	1 green pepper, cored, seeded and finely chopped
1 × 15 ml spoon brown sugar	1 tablespoon brown sugar
1 × 15 ml spoon vinegar	1 tablespoon vinegar
2 × 15 ml spoons soy sauce	2 tablespoons soy sauce
1 × 15 ml spoon cornflour	1 tablespoon cornflour
100 g button mushrooms, sliced if large	4 oz button mushrooms, sliced if large
salt	salt
freshly ground black pepper	freshly ground black pepper

Cooking time: about 35 minutes

Melt the butter in a large frying pan, add the chicken and fry over brisk heat until lightly coloured. Drain the pineapple and make up the juice to 220 ml/7 fl oz with water. Chop the pineapple slices roughly. Stir the green pepper, sugar, vinegar and soy sauce into the pineapple juice and add to the pan. Bring to the boil, stirring constantly, lower the heat, cover with foil and simmer for 15 to 20 minutes until the chicken is tender.
Mix the cornflour to a paste with a little water. Add to the pan and stir in well, then cook until the sauce thickens, stirring constantly. Add the chopped pineapple and the mushrooms and heat through for 5 minutes. Taste and adjust seasoning. Serve hot with freshly boiled noodles.

Italian pasta pot; Sweet and sour chicken

Crofter's pie

Metric	Imperial
2 × 15 ml spoons vegetable oil	2 tablespoons vegetable oil
1 onion, peeled and finely chopped	1 onion, peeled and finely chopped
few celery sticks, finely chopped	few celery sticks, finely chopped
750 g minced beef	1½ lb minced beef
1 × 400 g can tomatoes	1 × 14 oz can tomatoes
2 × 15 ml spoons tomato ketchup	2 tablespoons tomato ketchup
2 × 15 ml spoons Worcestershire sauce	2 tablespoons Worcestershire sauce
1 × 2.5 ml spoon mixed dried herbs	½ teaspoon mixed dried herbs
salt	salt
freshly ground black pepper	freshly ground black pepper
1 × 425 g can carrots, drained and roughly chopped	1 × 15 oz can carrots, drained and roughly chopped
1 × 100 g packet instant mashed potato mix	1 × 4 oz packet instant mashed potato mix
600 ml boiling water	1 pint boiling water
1 large knob of butter	1 large knob of butter

Cooking time: 45 minutes

Heat the oil in a large shallow pan, add the onion and celery, fry over gentle heat until soft. Add the meat and fry until browned, breaking it up constantly with a spoon. Stir in the tomatoes, tomato ketchup, Worcestershire sauce, herbs and salt and pepper to taste, then bring to the boil. Lower the heat and stir in half the carrots. Simmer for 25 minutes, taste and adjust seasoning.

Make the potato mix with the water according to packet directions, beat in the butter and salt and pepper to taste. Fold in the remaining carrots until evenly mixed, and spread on top of the meat mixture. Put under a very low grill for 10 minutes, turning the pan occasionally to ensure even browning.

Serve hot with a seasonal green vegetable or baked beans.

Crab pancakes

Metric	*Imperial*
2–3 large crabs	*2–3 large crabs*
1 × 175 g packet pancake	*1 × 6 oz packet pancake*
and batter mix	*and batter mix*
about 350 ml milk or water	*about 12 fl oz milk or water*
25 g lard	*1 oz lard*
1 × 300 ml packet cheese	*1 × ½ pint packet cheese*
sauce mix	*sauce mix*
300 ml milk	*½ pint milk*
pinch of cayenne pepper	*pinch of cayenne pepper*
salt	*salt*
freshly ground black pepper	*freshly ground black pepper*
1 large knob of butter	*1 large knob of butter*
4 × 15 ml spoons grated	*4 tablespoons grated*
Parmesan cheese	*Parmesan cheese*

Cooking time: about 40 minutes

Remove the meat from the crabs and flake with a fork, discarding any bones. Mix the white and dark meat together, then set aside. Make the batter with milk or water according to packet directions. Fry 8 pancakes in the hot lard.

Make the cheese sauce with the milk according to packet directions, add the cayenne and salt and pepper to taste. Mix a little of the cheese sauce into the crabmeat, divide equally between the pancakes and roll up.

Melt the butter in a large frying pan, add the pancakes and spread with the remaining cheese sauce. Cover with foil, then cook over gentle heat for 10 to 15 minutes until hot. Sprinkle with the Parmesan, put under a very low grill for 10 minutes until golden brown, turning the pan occasionally to ensure even browning. Serve immediately with a tomato and onion salad.

Variations:
Substitute 2 × 200 g/7 oz cans tuna or salmon for the crab, or use half fresh crab and half canned fish, depending on the availability and price of the crabs.

From left: Crofter's pie; Crab pancakes

Cheeseburgers

Metric
750 g minced beef
1 onion, peeled and very
    finely chopped
1 × 5 ml spoon mixed dried
    herbs
2 × 15 ml spoons
    Worcestershire sauce
pinch of mustard powder
salt
freshly ground black pepper
1 egg, beaten
4 × 15 ml spoons vegetable
    oil
6 slices Edam cheese
6 baps
butter for spreading

Imperial
1½ lb minced beef
1 onion, peeled and very
    finely chopped
1 teaspoon mixed dried
    herbs
2 tablespoons
    Worcestershire sauce
pinch of mustard powder
salt
freshly ground black pepper
1 egg, beaten
4 tablespoons vegetable
    oil
6 slices Edam cheese
6 baps
butter for spreading

Cooking time: about 20 minutes

Put the beef in a bowl with the onion, herbs, Worcestershire sauce, mustard and salt and pepper to taste. Mix well, then stir in the egg. Divide the mixture into 6 equal portions and form into hamburger shapes with the hands. Heat the oil in a large frying pan, add the hamburgers and fry for 7 minutes on each side until cooked through. Place a slice of cheese on top of each hamburger and put under a hot grill for 5 minutes until bubbling. Serve between buttered baps with sliced tomato, cucumber, shredded lettuce and potato crisps. Hand ketchup, relish, mustard and mayonnaise separately.
Makes 6 large hamburgers

Variations:
If you have a barbecue, then the burning charcoal will give the hamburgers a superb flavour. Cook them for the same length of time as above, but omit the cheese.

From front: Courgette moussaka; Cheeseburgers; Swiss potato cake

Swiss potato cake

Metric	Imperial
1 kg medium potatoes, peeled and cut in half	2 lb medium potatoes, peeled and cut in half
salt	salt
100 g Gruyère cheese	4 oz Gruyère cheese
freshly ground black pepper	freshly ground black pepper
1 large knob of butter	1 large knob of butter
1 small onion, peeled and finely chopped	1 small onion, peeled and finely chopped
4 back bacon rashers, de-rinded and cut into thin strips	4 back bacon rashers, de-rinded and cut into thin strips

Cooking time: about 35 minutes

This crisply fried potato cake makes a substantial brunch dish when served with fried eggs and sausages.

Cook the potatoes in boiling salted water for 10 minutes, drain and rinse under cold running water. Leave until cool enough to handle, then grate into a bowl. Grate in the cheese, add salt and pepper to taste and stir gently to mix.
Melt the butter in a frying pan, add the onion and bacon and fry over gentle heat until soft. Add the potato mixture, flatten it into a cake shape with a spatula and smooth the top. Fry over moderate heat for 10 minutes until crisp and brown underneath. Invert a plate over the pan and turn the cake out onto the plate. Slide the cake back into the pan and fry for a further 10 minutes until crisp and brown on the underside. Cut into wedges to serve.

Variation:
For a lighter and less expensive version, omit the bacon and use Edam or Gouda cheese.

Courgette moussaka

Metric	Imperial
8 × 15 ml spoons vegetable oil	8 tablespoons vegetable oil
1 onion, peeled and finely chopped	1 onion, peeled and finely chopped
1 garlic clove, peeled and crushed	1 garlic clove, peeled and crushed
750 g minced beef	1½ lb minced beef
3 × 15 ml spoons tomato purée	3 tablespoons tomato purée
1 × 5 ml spoon ground allspice	1 teaspoon ground allspice
pinch of mixed dried herbs	pinch of mixed dried herbs
5 × 15 ml spoons water	5 tablespoons water
salt	salt
freshly ground black pepper	freshly ground black pepper
500 g courgettes, sliced	1 lb courgettes, sliced
1 × 500 g can new potatoes, drained and sliced	1 × 1 lb can new potatoes, drained and sliced
1 × 300 ml packet cheese sauce mix	1 × ½ pint packet cheese sauce mix
300 ml milk	½ pint milk
1 egg	1 egg

Cooking time: about 50 minutes

Heat 2 × 15 ml spoons/2 tablespoons of the oil in a large shallow pan, add the onion and garlic and fry over gentle heat until soft. Add the meat and fry until browned, breaking it up constantly with a spoon. Stir in the tomato purée, allspice, herbs, water and salt and pepper to taste, then bring to the boil, stirring constantly. Lower the heat and simmer for 25 minutes.
Meanwhile, heat half the remaining oil in a frying pan, add some of the courgettes and fry gently until golden brown on both sides, drain. Fry the remaining courgettes in the same way, adding more oil when necessary.
Put the courgettes in a thick layer on top of the meat mixture, then cover with a layer of potatoes. Make the cheese sauce with the milk according to packet directions, leave to cool for a few minutes, then beat in the egg and salt and pepper to taste. Pour over the potatoes, put under a very low grill for 10 minutes, turning the pan occasionally to ensure even browning. Serve hot with a selection of salads and crusty French bread.

Variations:
Substitute sliced fried aubergines for the courgettes. The potatoes can be omitted for a less substantial dish, or they can be used on their own without either courgettes or aubergines.

Macaroni cheese

Metric	Imperial
6 large handfuls (300 ml) quick cooking macaroni	6 large handfuls (½ pint) quick cooking macaroni
salt	salt
1 knob of butter	1 knob of butter
1 onion, peeled and finely chopped	1 onion, peeled and finely chopped
4 back bacon rashers, de-rinded and chopped	4 back bacon rashers, de-rinded and chopped
1 × 300 ml packet cheese sauce mix	1 × ½ pint packet cheese sauce mix
300 ml milk	½ pint milk
freshly ground black pepper	freshly ground black pepper
100 g Cheddar cheese	4 oz Cheddar cheese
3 × 15 ml spoons golden breadcrumbs	3 tablespoons golden breadcrumbs
2 tomatoes, quartered	2 tomatoes, quartered

Cooking time: 25 minutes

Cook the macaroni in boiling salted water until tender according to packet directions. Meanwhile, melt the butter in a large shallow pan, add the onion and bacon and fry over gentle heat for 5 minutes, stirring occasionally. Mix the sauce mix with the milk according to packet directions, pour into the pan. Bring to the boil, stirring constantly, lower the heat and simmer until the sauce thickens. Add salt and pepper to taste.

Drain the macaroni thoroughly and stir into the pan. Grate the cheese over the top and sprinkle over the breadcrumbs. Arrange the tomatoes around the edge of the pan. Put under a hot grill for about 10 minutes until golden brown, turning the pan occasionally to ensure even browning. Serve hot with frankfurters, fried sausages or hamburgers, etc.

Variations:
Add 100 g/4 oz chopped mushrooms to the cheese sauce, or substitute 100 g/4 oz chopped garlic or ham sausage for the bacon.

Ham and vegetables au gratin

Metric	Imperial
2 large knobs of butter	2 large knobs of butter
1 large onion, peeled and sliced into rings	1 large onion, peeled and sliced into rings
225 g mushrooms, finely sliced	½ lb mushrooms, finely sliced
1 kg potatoes, peeled and very thinly sliced	2 lb potatoes, peeled and very thinly sliced
salt	salt
freshly ground black pepper	freshly ground black pepper
4 thick slices of boiled ham, cut into chunks	4 thick slices of boiled ham, cut into chunks
1 × 300 ml packet country herb sauce mix	1 × 2 pint packet country herb sauce mix
300 ml milk	½ pint milk
3–4 × 15 ml spoons golden breadcrumbs	3–4 tablespoons golden breadcrumbs

Cooking time: 55 minutes

Melt half the butter in a large frying pan, add the onion and fry over gentle heat until soft. Add the mushrooms and fry for 5 minutes, stirring constantly. Remove from the pan and set aside. Melt the remaining butter in the pan, then remove from the heat. Put a layer of potatoes in the bottom of the pan and sprinkle with salt and pepper. Cover with a layer of onion and mushrooms, then with some of the ham. Repeat these layers until all the ingredients are used up, finishing with a layer of potatoes. Return the pan to a very low heat.

Make the sauce with the milk according to packet directions, then pour over the potatoes. Cover loosely with foil and cook over very low heat for about 35 minutes or until the potatoes are tender. Remove the foil and sprinkle the breadcrumbs over the top. Put under a hot grill for 10 minutes, turning the pan occasionally to ensure even browning. Serve hot.

Variations:
Any kind of cooked or canned meat can be used instead of the boiled ham.
If liked, the ham can be omitted and the vegetable dish served with chops, steaks, gammon or cold meat.

From front: Ham and vegetables au gratin; Macaroni cheese; Devilled sausages and kidneys

Devilled sausages and kidneys

Metric
4 × 15 ml spoons vegetable oil
350 g skinless pork sausages, cut into chunks
1 onion, peeled and finely chopped
few celery sticks, finely chopped
225 g lamb's kidneys, skin and cores removed, sliced
2 × 15 ml spoons flour
225 ml water
1 beef stock cube
1 × 5 ml spoon prepared French mustard
2 × 15 ml spoons Worcestershire sauce
salt
freshly ground black pepper

Imperial
4 tablespoons vegetable oil
¾ lb skinless pork sausages, cut into chunks
1 onion, peeled and finely chopped
few celery sticks, finely chopped
8 oz lamb's kidneys, skin and cores removed, sliced
2 tablespoons flour
7 fl oz water
1 beef stock cube
1 teaspoon prepared French mustard
2 tablespoons Worcestershire sauce
salt
freshly ground black pepper

Cooking time: about 35 minutes

Heat half the oil in a small frying pan, add the sausages and fry until golden brown on all sides, shaking the pan occasionally. Remove from the pan with a slotted spoon and set aside. Heat the remaining oil in a large frying pan, add the onion and celery and fry over gentle heat for 10 minutes, stirring occasionally.

Add the kidneys and fry for 5 minutes until lightly coloured on all sides, stir in the flour and fry for a further 5 minutes. Stir in the water gradually, bring to the boil, add the stock cube and stir to dissolve. Add the sausages, mustard, Worcestershire sauce and salt and pepper to taste, lower the heat and simmer for 5 minutes or until the kidneys are tender. Taste and adjust seasoning. Serve hot on a bed of boiled rice.

57

From left: Fish pie mornay; Eggs in a nest; Caramel plum
charlotte; Spanish fish

Fish pie mornay

Metric	Imperial
2 knobs of butter	2 knobs of butter
500 g white fish fillets, skinned and cut into pieces	1 lb white fish fillets, skinned and cut into pieces
1 × 300 ml packet cheese sauce mix	1 × ½ pint packet cheese sauce mix
about 300 ml milk	about ½ pint milk
pinch of cayenne pepper	pinch of cayenne pepper
salt	salt
freshly ground black pepper	freshly ground black pepper
100 g peeled prawns	4 oz peeled prawns
1 × 100 g packet instant mashed potato mix	1 × 4 oz packet instant mashed potato mix
450 ml boiling water	¾ pint boiling water
3 hard-boiled eggs, sliced	3 hard-boiled eggs, sliced

Cooking time: about 30 minutes

Melt half the butter in a large shallow pan, add the
white fish and fry over gentle heat until lightly
coloured. Remove from the pan and drain off any
excess liquid. Mix the sauce mix with the milk
according to packet directions, then pour into the pan.
Bring to the boil, stirring occasionally, lower the heat
and cook until thick. Return the fish to the pan, add
the cayenne and salt and pepper to taste, cook gently
for 10 minutes. Add the prawns and cook for a further
5 minutes.
Make the potato mix with the water according to
packet directions. Arrange the eggs over the fish
mixture, cover with the potato and mark with a fork.
Dot with the remaining butter, put under a hot grill
for 10 minutes until browned, turning the pan
occasionally to ensure even browning. Serve hot with
French beans or peas.

Eggs in a nest

Metric	Imperial
600 ml water	1 pint water
2 knobs of butter	2 knobs of butter
3 eggs	3 eggs
1 × 425 g can baked beans	1 × 15 oz can baked beans
1 × 100 g packet instant mashed potato mix	1 × 4 oz packet instant mashed potato mix
salt	salt
freshly ground black pepper	freshly ground black pepper
approximately 75 g Cheddar cheese	approximately 3 oz Cheddar cheese

Cooking time: about 15 minutes

You will need a stacking set with an egg poacher.

Heat the water in the large shallow pan of the stacking
set. Put the egg poacher on the top and divide 1 knob
of butter equally between the poaching cups. Crack
in the eggs, cover with a lid and poach over gentle
heat for 5 minutes.
Meanwhile, put the baked beans in a separate pan
and heat gently. Remove the egg poacher with the lid
and set aside. Sprinkle the potato mix over the water
in the bottom pan, beat until smooth. Add the remaining butter and salt and pepper to taste.
Spread the potato around the outside of the pan to
make the nest, then pour the baked beans into the
centre. Slide the eggs on top of the beans and grate
the cheese on top. Put under a hot grill for 5 minutes
until the cheese melts.
Serves 3

Caramel plum charlotte

Metric
2 × 500 g cans plums in
  syrup
1 × 5 ml spoon ground
  cinnamon
finely grated rind of
  1 orange
finely grated rind of
  1 lemon
5–6 thick slices of brown
  bread, crusts removed
butter for spreading
6 × 15 ml spoons soft brown
  sugar

Imperial
2 × 1 lb cans plums in
  syrup
1 teaspoon ground
  cinnamon
finely grated rind of
  1 orange
finely grated rind of
  1 lemon
5–6 thick slices of brown
  bread, crusts removed
butter for spreading
6 tablespoons soft brown
  sugar

Cooking time: 20 minutes

Put 1 can of plums in a large shallow pan. Drain off the juice from the remaining can, then add to the plums in the pan. Sprinkle with the cinnamon and orange and lemon rinds.

Meanwhile, spread the bread thickly with butter and cut each slice in half. Arrange on top of the plums butter side up, to cover them completely, then sprinkle over the sugar. Put under a low to moderate grill for about 10 minutes until the sugar has caramelized, turning the pan occasionally to ensure even browning. Remove from the grill and leave to cool for 5 minutes. Serve lukewarm with fresh cream or ice cream.

Variations:
Use canned gooseberries or rhubarb instead of the plums. Or use 1 kg/2 lb fresh fruit and poach it with sugar first.

Spanish fish

Metric
2 × 15 ml spoons olive oil
1 small onion, peeled
  and finely chopped
1 garlic clove, peeled
  and finely chopped
2 small green or red peppers,
  cored, seeded and
  finely chopped
1 × 400 g can tomatoes
1 × 2.5 ml spoon dried
  tarragon
salt
freshly ground black pepper
2 knobs of butter
4 large white fish
  fillets, skinned

Imperial
2 tablespoons olive oil
1 small onion, peeled
  and finely chopped
1 garlic clove, peeled
  and finely chopped
2 small green or red peppers,
  cored, seeded and
  finely chopped
1 × 14 oz can tomatoes
½ teaspoon dried
  tarragon
salt
freshly ground black pepper
2 knobs of butter
4 large white fish
  fillets, skinned

Cooking time: 40 minutes

Heat the oil in a pan, add the onion, garlic and peppers and fry over gentle heat for 10 minutes. Add the tomatoes, break up with a spoon, then stir in the tarragon and salt and pepper to taste. Bring to the boil, lower the heat and simmer for 20 minutes, stirring occasionally.

Meanwhile, melt the butter in a separate pan, add the fish and fry over gentle heat for 5 minutes on each side. Pour the onion and pepper mixture over the fish, then continue cooking for a further 10 minutes. Taste and adjust seasoning. Serve hot with crusty French bread or mashed potato.

THE PRESSURE COOKER

Many camping and boating enthusiasts consider a pressure cooker to be their most important piece of cooking equipment. If you are used to cooking with a pressure cooker, then you will certainly find it indispensable on this type of holiday, although perhaps it would be wiser not to take one with you unless you have mastered the art of using it at home. There is no doubt that a pressure cooker will save not only your own valuable time while on holiday, but it will also save on fuel – a beef casserole can cook in 15 minutes rather than 2 hours, for example. If you use the special trivets and baskets provided, you can also save on washing up by cooking meat and vegetables together in one pan.

If you are considering buying a pressure cooker, then the best kind to choose is the kind without a long handle, because this could so easily be knocked off the cooker in the confines of a tent awning, caravan or boat. There is now available a pressure cooker which has two short handles, one on each side, thus making it more stable and therefore most suitable for camping.

There are a few points to bear in mind when using a pressure cooker on a camping holiday:

1. Always read the manufacturer's instructions carefully and follow them to the letter.
2. Never leave the pressure cooker unattended in a tent awning, caravan or boat.
3. Check the gasket and safety plug before going away and take spares with you.
4. Be prepared for a steamy atmosphere if you are pressure cooking in a restricted space.

Note : H (high) pressure equals 15 lb in weight on the pressure cooker.

Pork chops with apple and cheese sauce

Metric	Imperial
4 pork chops, rind and fat removed	4 pork chops, rind and fat removed
2 × 5 ml spoons prepared French mustard, or to taste	2 teaspoons prepared French mustard, or to taste
salt	salt
freshly ground black pepper	freshly ground black pepper
2 × 15 ml spoons vegetable oil	2 tablespoons vegetable oil
2 large cooking apples, cored, seeded and thickly sliced	2 large cooking apples, cored, seeded and thickly sliced
100 g Cheddar cheese	4 oz Cheddar cheese
150 ml chicken stock	¼ pint chicken stock

H pressure: 10 minutes

Spread the chops with the mustard and sprinkle liberally with salt and pepper. Heat the oil in the pressure cooker, add the chops and fry over brisk heat until browned on both sides. Cover the chops with the apples and grate the cheese over the top. Pour in the stock and bring to the boil. Cover with the lid, then bring up to pressure according to manufacturer's instructions. Cook at H pressure for 10 minutes, then reduce the pressure quickly and remove the cover. Taste and adjust the seasoning. Serve hot with seasonal vegetables.

Pork chops with apple and cheese sauce; Summer pot roast

Summer pot roast

Metric
1 × 1½ kg joint brisket
  or topside of beef
2 × 15 ml spoons flour
salt
freshly ground black pepper
2 × 15 ml spoons vegetable
  oil
1 onion, peeled and
  finely chopped
2 garlic cloves, peeled
  and crushed
few celery sticks
4 streaky bacon rashers,
  de-rinded and chopped
1 × 400 g can tomatoes
150 ml red wine
150 ml water
1 × 2.5 ml spoon dried
  basil or oregano
4 medium potatoes, peeled
  and quartered
cornflour, to thicken
  (optional)

Imperial
1 × 3 lb joint brisket
  or topside of beef
2 tablespoons flour
salt
freshly ground black pepper
2 tablespoons vegetable
  oil
1 onion, peeled and
  finely chopped
2 garlic cloves, peeled
  and crushed
few celery sticks
4 streaky bacon rashers,
  de-rinded and chopped
1 × 14 oz can tomatoes
¼ pint red wine
¼ pint water
½ teaspoon dried
  basil or oregano
4 medium potatoes, peeled
  and quartered
cornflour, to thicken
  (optional)

H Pressure: 60 minutes

Calculate the cooking time at 20 minutes per 500 g/ 1 lb meat.

Sprinkle the beef with the flour seasoned with salt and pepper. Heat the oil in the pressure cooker, add the beef and fry over brisk heat until browned on all sides. Remove from the cooker and set aside. Add the onion, garlic, celery and bacon and fry over gentle heat until lightly coloured. Stir in the tomatoes, wine and water, add the basil or oregano and salt and pepper to taste and bring to the boil.

Place the trivet in the cooker, rim side down. Put the beef on the trivet. Cover with the lid, bring up to pressure according to manufacturer's instructions. Cook at H pressure for 55 minutes, reduce the pressure quickly, remove the cover and add the potatoes. Close the cooker again, bring back to pressure and cook for a further 5 minutes. Reduce the pressure quickly and remove the cover.

Lift out the beef and potatoes and keep hot. Remove the trivet, taste and adjust the seasoning of the sauce. Thicken the sauce, if liked, by mixing cornflour to a paste with a little water, stir into the sauce and return to the heat. Bring to the boil, stirring constantly, and cook until the sauce thickens. Slice the beef and serve hot with a seasonal vegetable.
Serves 4 to 6

Variations:
Substitute white wine or dry cider for the red wine, or simply use beef stock made with a stock cube.

Beef, bacon and bean hotpot

Metric	Imperial
2 × 15 ml spoons vegetable oil	2 tablespoons vegetable oil
1 large onion, peeled and finely chopped	1 large onion, peeled and finely chopped
1 garlic clove, peeled and crushed	1 garlic clove, peeled and crushed
750 g chuck steak, cut into 2.5 cm chunks	1½ lb chuck steak, cut into 1 inch chunks
225 g streaky bacon, de-rinded and chopped	8 oz streaky bacon, de-rinded and chopped
1 × 400 g can tomatoes	1 × 14 oz can tomatoes
2 × 15 ml spoons tomato purée	2 tablespoons tomato purée
2 × 5 ml spoons prepared French mustard	2 teaspoons prepared French mustard
1 × 15 ml spoon black treacle, brown sugar or golden syrup	1 tablespoon black treacle, brown sugar or golden syrup
150 ml water	¼ pint water
6 handfuls (scant 300 ml) red kidney beans, soaked overnight and drained	6 handfuls (scant ½ pint) red kidney beans, soaked overnight and drained
salt	salt
freshly ground black pepper	freshly ground black pepper

H pressure: 20 minutes

Heat the oil in the pressure cooker, add the onion and fry over gentle heat until soft. Add the garlic, beef and bacon, then fry over brisk heat until the meat is browned on all sides. Stir in the water, tomatoes, tomato purée, mustard, treacle and beans, then add salt and pepper to taste. Bring to the boil.
Cover with the lid and bring up to pressure according to manufacturer's instructions. Cook at H pressure for 20 minutes, reduce the pressure quickly and remove the cover. Taste and adjust the seasoning. Serve hot with freshly boiled rice.
Serves 4 to 6

Variation:
Substitute dried haricot beans for the kidney beans.

From left: Pork, ginger and apple hotpot; Beef, bacon and bean hotpot Chinese pork with mushrooms

Pork, ginger and apple hotpot

Metric	Imperial
750 g boned shoulder or sparerib of pork, cut into chunks	1½ lb boned shoulder or sparerib of pork, cut into chunks
2 × 15 ml spoons flour	2 tablespoons flour
salt	salt
freshly ground black pepper	freshly ground black pepper
2 × 15 ml spoons vegetable oil	2 tablespoons vegetable oil
1 kg potatoes, peeled and thickly sliced	2 lb potatoes, peeled and thickly sliced
2–3 large cooking apples, peeled, cored and thickly sliced	2–3 large cooking apples, peeled, cored and thickly sliced
1 onion, peeled and thinly sliced	1 onion, peeled and thinly sliced
1 × 5 ml spoon ground ginger	1 teaspoon ground ginger
300 ml dry cider	½ pint dry cider

H pressure: 15 minutes

Coat the pork in the flour seasoned with salt and pepper. Heat the oil in the pressure cooker, add the pork and fry over brisk heat until browned on all sides. Remove from the cooker. Put the potatoes, apples, onion and pork in layers in the cooker, sprinkling each layer with the ginger and salt and pepper. Pour in the cider and bring to the boil. Cover with the lid, then bring up to pressure according to manufacturer's instructions. Cook at H pressure for 15 minutes, then reduce the pressure quickly and remove the cover. Serve hot with a seasonal green vegetable.

Chinese pork
with mushrooms

Metric
750 g boned shoulder or
  sparerib of pork, cut
  into 2.5 cm chunks
3 × 15 ml spoons soy sauce
2 × 15 ml spoons
  cornflour
2 garlic cloves, peeled
  and crushed
1 × 5 ml spoon ground
  ginger
freshly ground black pepper
2 × 15 ml spoons vegetable
  oil
1 bunch of spring onions,
  trimmed and chopped
450 ml water
1 chicken stock cube
100 g button mushrooms,
  sliced if large
50 g salted cashew nuts

Imperial
1½ lb boned shoulder or
  sparerib of pork, cut
  into 1 inch chunks
3 tablespoons soy sauce
2 tablespoons
  cornflour
2 garlic cloves, peeled
  and crushed
1 teaspoon ground
  ginger
freshly ground black pepper
2 tablespoons vegetable
  oil
1 bunch of spring onions,
  trimmed and chopped
¾ pint water
1 chicken stock cube
4 oz button mushrooms,
  sliced if large
2 oz salted cashew nuts

H pressure: 15 minutes

Put the pork in a bowl with the soy sauce, cornflour, garlic, ginger and pepper to taste. Stir well to mix. Heat the oil in the pressure cooker, add the onions and fry over gentle heat for 5 minutes. Add the pork and fry over brisk heat until browned on all sides, stirring constantly. Stir in the water and scrape up the sediment from the bottom of the cooker, then bring to the boil. Add the stock cube and stir to dissolve.

Cover with the lid, then bring up to pressure according to manufacturer's instructions. Cook at H pressure for 10 minutes, reduce the pressure quickly, remove the cover and add the mushrooms and cashew nuts. Cover the cooker again, bring back to pressure and cook for a further 5 minutes.

Reduce the pressure quickly and remove the cover. Taste and adjust the seasoning, adding more soy sauce and ginger if a stronger flavour is liked. Serve hot with freshly boiled rice or noodles and fresh or canned bean sprouts.

Variations:
Use 2 green peppers, cored, seeded and finely chopped, instead of the mushrooms.
Substitute 4 boned chicken breasts, skinned and sliced, for the pork. Cook for 5 minutes at H pressure.

Rogan gosht

Metric	Imperial
2 × 15 ml spoons vegetable oil	2 tablespoons vegetable oil
1 large onion, peeled and finely chopped	1 large onion, peeled and finely chopped
1 garlic clove, peeled and crushed	1 garlic clove, peeled and crushed
2 × 15 ml spoons curry paste	2 tablespoons curry paste
1 × 2.5 ml spoon chilli powder, or to taste	½ teaspoon chilli powder, or to taste
750 g chuck steak, cut into 2.5 cm chunks	1½ lb chuck steak, cut into 1 inch chunks
2 × 15 ml spoons flour	2 tablespoons flour
salt	salt
freshly ground black pepper	freshly ground black pepper
300 ml water	½ pint water
1 × 15 ml spoon vinegar	1 tablespoon vinegar
1 beef stock cube	1 beef stock cube
2 green or red peppers, cored, seeded and chopped	2 green or red peppers, cored, seeded and chopped
4 tomatoes, quartered	4 tomatoes, quartered
cornflour, to thicken (optional)	cornflour, to thicken (optional)

H Pressure: 20 minutes

This is a beef curry with tomatoes and peppers. Add the chilli powder with care – it is a very hot spice.

Heat the oil in the pressure cooker, add the onion and fry over gentle heat until soft. Add the garlic, curry paste and chilli powder and fry for 5 minutes, stirring constantly.

Meanwhile, coat the beef in the flour seasoned with salt and pepper. Add to the cooker and fry over brisk heat until browned on all sides. Stir in the water and vinegar and scrape up the sediment from the bottom of the cooker, then bring to the boil. Add the stock cube and stir to dissolve.

Cover with the lid, then bring up to pressure according to manufacturer's instructions. Cook at H pressure for 15 minutes. Reduce the pressure quickly, remove the cover and add the peppers and tomatoes. Cover the cooker again, bring back to pressure and cook for a further 5 minutes. Reduce the pressure quickly and remove the cover. Taste and adjust the seasoning of the sauce. Thicken, if liked, by mixing cornflour to a paste with a little water, stir into the sauce and return to the heat. Bring to the boil, stirring constantly, and cook until the sauce thickens. Serve hot with freshly boiled rice, mango chutney and plain yogurt.

Gammon with apricots

Metric	Imperial
1 × 1½ kg unsmoked gammon joint	1 × 3 lb unsmoked gammon joint
1 knob of butter	1 knob of butter
2 × 15 ml spoons brown sugar	2 tablespoons brown sugar
1 × 2.5 ml spoon ground allspice or mixed spice	½ teaspoon ground allspice or mixed spice
150 ml undiluted orange squash	¼ pint undiluted orange squash
150 ml water	¼ pint water
100 g dried apricots, soaked overnight and drained	4 oz dried apricots, soaked overnight and drained
2 × 5 ml spoons arrowroot	2 teaspoons arrowroot

H pressure: 35 minutes

Cook at 12 minutes per 500 g/1 lb at H pressure.

Put the gammon in the pressure cooker and cover with water. Bring to the boil, remove the gammon and discard the water. Put the trivet in the cooker, rim side down. Place the gammon on the trivet, rind uppermost. Add 750 ml/1¼ pints water, bring to the boil and skim with a slotted spoon. Cover with the lid and bring up to pressure according to manufacturer's instructions.

Cook at H pressure for 30 minutes, reduce the pressure quickly and remove the cover. Drain the gammon, cut off the skin and fat. Melt the butter in the cooker, add the sugar and allspice or mixed spice and fry over gentle heat for 1–2 minutes, stirring. Stir in the orange squash and water, return the gammon to the cooker and place the apricots on top. Cover the cooker again, bring back to pressure and cook for a further 5 minutes. Reduce the pressure quickly and remove the cover. Lift out the gammon and apricots and keep hot. Mix the arrowroot to a paste with a little water, stir into the sauce and return to the heat. Bring to the boil, stirring constantly, and cook until the sauce thickens. Slice the gammon, add the apricots to the sauce and serve hot.

Gammon with apricots; Rogan gosht

OVEN MEALS

If you have bought or hired a caravan or boat with a built-in oven, or have had one fitted in yourself, then you will obviously want to take full advantage of this very useful additional cooking medium. There is no doubt that the oven will widen your scope and choice of dishes, but at the same time it is essential to realize the limitations of this type of oven. Firstly, it would be pointless to attempt to cook any dish that requires a precise oven temperature, because the camping oven can only give approximate temperatures, usually the regulo gives only low, medium and high. Secondly, the oven is much smaller than a normal domestic oven and you must always watch carefully to see that the food does not become overcooked, or even burnt, immediately above the burners at the back. For this reason it is hardly worth trying to bake a cake, for example, as the constant opening of the oven door would cause it to sink. However, if you cook the dishes that are in this chapter, or at least try to keep to this type of dish, you should find your oven well worth having.

Savoury meat loaf; Cheesy garlic bread

Cheesy garlic bread

Metric
1 Vienna loaf or small French stick
75 g butter, softened
1–2 garlic cloves, peeled and crushed
salt
freshly ground black pepper
75 g cream cheese with chives

Imperial
1 Vienna loaf or small French stick
3 oz butter, softened
1–2 garlic cloves, peeled and crushed
salt
freshly ground black pepper
3 oz cream cheese with chives

Oven cooking time: 20 minutes

Preheat the oven at high temperature for 5 minutes. Meanwhile, cut the bread into thick slices without cutting right through the base. Cream the butter and garlic together with salt and pepper to taste, then spread on the cut surfaces of the bread. Spread the cream cheese on top of the butter. Wrap in foil, then bake in the centre of the oven for 15 minutes. Open the foil wrapping, then bake for a further 5 minutes, or until the bread is crisp. Serve hot with main courses as a substitute for potatoes, noodles or rice.

Savoury meat loaf

Metric
225 g minced beef
225 g minced pork
1 × 75 g packet sage and onion stuffing mix
2 eating apples, peeled
1 egg, beaten
4 × 15 ml spoons hot water
salt
freshly ground black pepper

Imperial
½ lb minced beef
½ lb minced pork
1 × 3 oz packet sage and onion stuffing mix
2 eating apples, peeled
1 egg, beaten
4 tablespoons hot water
salt
freshly ground black pepper

Oven cooking time: 1 hour

Preheat the oven at medium temperature for 5 minutes. Put the beef, pork and stuffing mix in a bowl. Grate the apple flesh into the bowl. Add the egg, water and salt and pepper, then stir well to mix.
Press the mixture into a greased 450 g/1 lb loaf tin or ovenproof dish and cover with foil. Bake in the centre of the oven for 1 hour, or until the juices run clear when the centre of the loaf is pierced with a skewer or knife. Remove the loaf from the oven, then leave to stand for 5 minutes. Drain off the excess fat and juices from the loaf, then turn the loaf out on to a serving dish and leave until cold. Cut into slices and serve with salads.

Variations:
Use all minced beef or pork, or a different stuffing mix. Sausage meat can also be used instead of the pork. Alternatively, serve hot with a tomato and mushroom sauce, boiled new potatoes and a seasonal vegetable.

Chicken parcels

Metric
1 large knob of butter
4 boned chicken breasts,
    skinned
1 × 400 g packet frozen
    puff pastry, thawed
salt
freshly ground black pepper
50 g liver sausage
1 small egg, beaten

Imperial
1 large knob of butter
4 boned chicken breasts,
    skinned
1 × 14 oz packet frozen
    puff pastry, thawed
salt
freshly ground black pepper
2 oz liver sausage
1 small egg, beaten

Oven cooking time: 15 minutes

Melt the butter in a frying pan, add the chicken and fry for 20 minutes, turning occasionally. Remove from the pan and leave until cool enough to handle. Meanwhile, roll out the pastry thinly and cut into 4 squares. Sprinkle the chicken pieces with salt and pepper. Spread the liver sausage on top of each piece, then place the chicken on the squares of pastry, with the liver sausage downwards. Wrap the pastry around the chicken to enclose it completely, then place in a roasting tin with the joins underneath.
Preheat the oven at high temperature for 5 minutes. Brush all over the pastry with the egg, then bake in the centre of the oven for 15 minutes or until golden brown. Serve hot with seasonal vegetables and gravy, or cold with a selection of salads.

Variations :
Substitute chutney, mustard or chopped cooked mushrooms for the liver sausage.

Chicken parcels

Baked stuffed mackerel

Baked stuffed mackerel

Oven cooking time: 30 minutes

Metric	Imperial
1 × 75 g packet parsley and thyme stuffing mix	*1 × 3 oz packet parsley and thyme stuffing mix*
about 150 ml hot water	*about ¼ pint hot water*
finely grated rind and juice of 1 lemon	*finely grated rind and juice of 1 lemon*
1 bunch of parsley, finely chopped	*1 bunch of parsley, finely chopped*
1 large knob of butter	*1 large knob of butter*
freshly ground black pepper	*freshly ground black pepper*
4 mackerel, cleaned and filleted	*4 mackerel, cleaned and filleted*

Put the stuffing mix in a bowl, add the water according to packet directions and stir well. Add the remaining ingredients except the mackerel and stir again. Lay the mackerel flat on a board, skin side down, then put the stuffing along the centre of each fish and wrap the fish around the stuffing to enclose it. Preheat the oven at medium temperature for 5 minutes. Place the fish in an ovenproof dish with the joins underneath, then cover with a sheet of buttered greaseproof paper or foil. Bake in the centre of the oven for 30 minutes, then serve hot with new potatoes and seasonal vegetables.

Variation:
Stuffed mackerel is also good served cold with mayonnaise and tomato salad.

Thatched meat loaf

Metric	Imperial
3 slices of bread, crusts removed, broken into pieces	3 slices of bread, crusts removed, broken into pieces
450 g minced beef	1 lb minced beef
1 onion, peeled and finely chopped	1 onion, peeled and finely chopped
2 × 15 ml spoons Worcestershire sauce	2 tablespoons Worcestershire sauce
1 egg, beaten	1 egg, beaten
1 × 5 ml spoon dried mixed herbs	1 teaspoon dried mixed herbs
salt	salt
freshly ground black pepper	freshly ground black pepper
1 × 100 g packet instant mashed potato mix	1 × 4 oz packet instant mashed potato mix
600 ml boiling water	1 pint of boiling water
1 knob of butter	1 knob of butter

Oven cooking time: 1 hour 20 minutes

Put the bread in a small bowl, then cover with water. Leave to stand for 10 minutes, then squeeze dry. Mix the bread with the beef, onion, Worcestershire sauce, egg, herbs and salt and pepper to taste.
Preheat the oven at medium temperature for 5 minutes. Press the mixture into a greased 450 g/1 lb loaf tin or ovenproof dish and cover with foil. Bake in the centre of the oven for 1 hour, or until the juices run clear when the centre of the loaf is pierced with a skewer or knife.
Remove the loaf from the oven and leave to stand in the tin or dish for 10 minutes. Meanwhile, make the potato mix with the water according to packet directions, then beat in the butter and salt and pepper to taste. Drain off the excess fat and juices from the loaf, then turn the loaf out on to a baking sheet. Spread the potato over the loaf to cover it completely, then rough up the surface with a fork.
Return to the oven and bake at high temperature for 20 minutes, turning the baking sheet round half way through cooking. Serve hot with seasonal vegetables or baked beans.

Variation:
Omit the potato topping and serve the meat loaf cold with salad – ideal for picnics.

Fish finger bake

Metric	Imperial
500 g frozen spinach, thawed	1 lb frozen spinach, thawed
salt	salt
freshly ground black pepper	freshly ground black pepper
16 frozen fish fingers	16 frozen fish fingers
vegetable oil or lard, for frying	vegetable oil or lard, for frying
1½ × 15 ml spoons cornflour	1½ tablespoons cornflour
450 ml milk	¾ pint milk
1 large knob of butter	1 large knob of butter
100 g Cheddar cheese	4 oz Cheddar cheese

Oven cooking time: 15 minutes

Preheat the oven at low temperature for 5 minutes. Put the spinach in the bottom of an ovenproof dish, sprinkle with salt and pepper, then put in the oven to heat through. Meanwhile, fry the fish fingers in hot oil or lard until crisp on both sides. Mix the cornflour to a paste with a little of the milk. Heat the remaining milk in a pan with the butter, then gradually stir in the cornflour paste. Bring to the boil and cook until the sauce thickens, stirring constantly. Remove from the heat, grate in half the cheese, then stir until melted. Add salt and pepper to taste.
Arrange the fish fingers on top of the spinach, then pour over the cheese sauce. Grate the remaining cheese over the top. Turn the oven up to medium temperature, then bake in the centre of the oven for 15 minutes until golden brown and bubbling. Serve immediately with boiled new potatoes or French bread.

Variations:
Substitute frozen cod or haddock steaks for the fish fingers.
If preferred, cheese sauce mix can be used instead of the milk, cornflour and cheese.

Thatched meat loaf; Fish finger bake

Six layer dinner

Metric	Imperial
2 large knobs of butter	2 large knobs of butter
1 large Spanish onion, peeled and finely sliced	1 large Spanish onion, peeled and finely sliced
450 g pork sausages	1 lb pork sausages
1 × 300 g can condensed tomato soup	1 × 10 oz can condensed tomato soup
1 × 75 g packet country stuffing mix	1 × 3 oz packet country stuffing mix
1 × 100 g packet frozen sweetcorn	1 × 4 oz packet frozen sweetcorn
1 × 100 g packet instant mashed potato mix	1 × 4 oz packet instant mashed potato mix
600 ml boiling water	1 pint boiling water
salt	salt
freshly ground black pepper	freshly ground black pepper

Oven cooking time: 30 minutes

Melt half the butter in a frying pan, add the onion and fry over gentle heat until soft and lightly coloured. Remove the onion with a slotted spoon and set aside. Add the sausages to the pan, fry until browned on all sides, then transfer to the bottom of an ovenproof dish. Cover with the onion, then the tomato soup. Sprinkle over half the stuffing mix, then the sweetcorn. Preheat the oven at medium temperature for 5 minutes. Make the potato mix with the water according to packet directions, then beat in the remaining butter and salt and pepper to taste. Spread over the ingredients in the dish, then sprinkle with the remaining stuffing mix. Bake in the centre of the oven for 30 minutes, then serve hot.

Variations :
Any vegetables can be used instead of the ones given here – try fresh tomatoes, frozen or canned peas, sliced canned carrots or baked beans.

Tuna Italian style

Metric	Imperial
6 handfuls (good 300 ml) quick-cooking macaroni	6 handfuls (good ½ pint) quick-cooking macaroni
salt	salt
1½ × 15 ml spoons cornflour	1½ tablespoons cornflour
450 ml milk	¾ pint milk
1 large knob of butter	1 large knob of butter
1 large bunch of parsley, finely chopped	1 large bunch of parsley, finely chopped
2 × 175 g cans tuna fish, drained and flaked	2 × 6 oz cans tuna fish, drained and flaked
freshly ground black pepper	freshly ground black pepper
3 tomatoes, sliced	3 tomatoes, sliced
1 small packet of plain crisps, crushed	1 small packet of plain crisps, crushed

Oven cooking time: 15 minutes

Cook the macaroni in boiling salted water until barely tender, according to packet directions. Drain thoroughly, then return to the pan. Mix the cornflour to a paste with a little of the milk. Heat the remaining milk and the butter in the pan with the macaroni, then gradually stir in the cornflour paste. Bring to the boil and cook until the sauce thickens, stirring constantly. Remove from the heat, then gently fold in the parsley and tuna. Add salt and pepper to taste.
Preheat the oven at high temperature for 5 minutes. Pour the mixture into an ovenproof dish and smooth the top. Arrange the tomato slices around the edge, then sprinkle the crisps in the centre. Bake in the centre of the oven for 15 minutes, then serve immediately with a tossed green salad or a seasonal vegetable.

Six layer dinner; Stuffed peppers; Tuna Italian style

Stuffed peppers

Metric	Imperial
4 green peppers, cored and seeded, tops reserved	4 green peppers, cored and seeded, tops reserved
2 × 15 ml spoons vegetable oil	2 tablespoons vegetable oil
1 onion, peeled and finely chopped	1 onion, peeled and finely chopped
225 g minced beef	½ lb minced beef
1 × 225 g can tomatoes	1 × 8 oz can tomatoes
2 × 15 ml spoons tomato purée	2 tablespoons tomato purée
1 × 5 ml spoon dried oregano	1 teaspoon dried oregano
salt	salt
freshly ground black pepper	freshly ground black pepper
100 g (142 ml) long-grain rice, cooked	4 oz (½ cup) long-grain rice, cooked

Oven cooking time: 40 minutes

Put the peppers in a bowl, cover with boiling water, then leave for at least 10 minutes. Meanwhile, heat the oil in a pan, add the onion and fry over gentle heat until soft. Add the meat and fry until browned, breaking it up constantly with a spoon. Stir in the remaining ingredients except the rice and bring to the boil. Simmer for 15 minutes until the liquid has reduced, then remove from the heat and stir in the rice.

Preheat the oven at medium temperature for 5 minutes. Drain the peppers then stand them in an ovenproof dish. Divide the meat and rice mixture equally between the peppers, spooning any surplus mixture around them. Put the tops on the peppers, then bake in the centre of the oven for 20 minutes. Transfer to the floor of the oven and bake for a further 20 minutes. Serve hot with a tomato sauce, mixed salad and garlic bread, if liked.

Variation:
Add 100 g/4 oz mushrooms, finely chopped, to the stuffing mixture and halve the quantity of rice.

Chicken, ham and mushroom pie

Metric	Imperial
1 knob of butter	1 knob of butter
100 g button mushrooms, sliced	4 oz button mushrooms, sliced
1 × 300 ml packet parsley sauce mix	1 × ½ pint packet parsley sauce mix
300 ml milk	½ pint milk
2 roasted chicken quarters, skinned, boned and cut into small chunks	2 roasted chicken quarters, skinned, boned and cut into small chunks
1 × 100 g piece boiled ham, fat removed and cut into small chunks	1 × 4 oz piece boiled ham, fat removed and cut into small chunks
freshly ground black pepper	freshly ground black pepper
1 × 225 g packet frozen puff pastry, thawed	1 × 8 oz packet frozen puff pastry, thawed
1 small egg, beaten	1 small egg, beaten

Oven cooking time: about 25 minutes

Melt the butter in a pan, add the mushrooms and fry over gentle heat for 5 minutes. Combine the parsley sauce mix and the milk according to packet directions, then add to the pan. Bring to the boil and cook until the sauce thickens, stirring constantly. Stir in the chicken and ham, and pepper to taste, then cook gently for 10 minutes, stirring occasionally. Meanwhile, preheat the oven at high temperature for 5 minutes.

Spoon the filling into a deep ovenproof pie dish. Roll out the pastry for the lid, moisten the rim of the dish and place the pastry over the filling. Seal the edges and brush all over the pastry with the egg. Make a small hole in the centre for the steam to escape and use any trimmings for decoration. Bake in the centre of the oven for about 25 minutes, turning the dish round half way through cooking. Cover the pastry with foil if it is becoming too brown. Leave to stand for 5 minutes before serving with seasonal vegetables or salads.

Variation:
Substitute frozen sweetcorn for the mushrooms, and white sauce mix seasoned with 1 × 2.5 ml/½ teaspoon paprika pepper, for the parsley sauce mix.

Sardine roll

Metric	Imperial
2 × 100 g cans sardines in oil, drained	2 × 4 oz cans sardines in oil, drained
2 tomatoes, finely chopped	2 tomatoes, finely chopped
1 garlic clove, peeled and crushed (optional)	1 garlic clove, peeled and crushed (optional)
1 × 15 ml spoon lemon juice	1 tablespoon lemon juice
freshly ground black pepper	freshly ground black pepper
1 × 400 g packet frozen puff pastry, thawed	1 × 14 oz packet frozen puff pastry, thawed
1 small egg, beaten	1 small egg, beaten

Oven cooking time: 20 minutes

Put the sardines in a bowl with the tomatoes, garlic (if using), lemon juice and plenty of black pepper. Mash the ingredients well together. Cut the pastry in two, then roll out each piece to an oblong about 25 × 15 cm/10 × 6 inches. Spread the sardine mixture over the two pieces of pastry, leaving a 1 cm/½ in margin around the edges.

Preheat the oven at high temperature for 5 minutes. Roll up each piece of pastry from the long end to form a Swiss roll shape, then cut each roll into about 10 slices. Stand the slices close together on a baking sheet, then brush all over with the egg. Bake in the centre of the oven for 20 minutes, turning the baking sheet round half way through cooking. Cover the slices with foil if they are becoming too brown. Leave to stand for 5 minutes before serving with a crisp green salad or a tomato and onion salad.

Variations:
Substitute a 200 g/7 oz can salmon, drained and boned, or a 225 g/8 oz can pilchards, drained, for the sardines.

Sardine roll; Chicken, ham and mushroom pie

Barbecued lamb chops

Oven cooking time: about 1 hour

Metric	Imperial
1 kg lamb chops, trimmed of fat	2 lb lamb chops, trimmed of fat
salt	salt
freshly ground black pepper	freshly ground black pepper
2 × 15 ml spoons honey	2 tablespoons honey
2 × 15 ml spoons soy sauce	2 tablespoons soy sauce
2 × 15 ml spoons tomato ketchup	2 tablespoons tomato ketchup
2 garlic cloves, peeled and crushed	2 garlic cloves, peeled and crushed
300 ml boiling water	½ pint boiling water
1 chicken stock cube	1 chicken stock cube
1 × 15 ml spoon cornflour	1 tablespoon cornflour

Preheat the oven at high temperature for 5 minutes. Put the chops in a roasting tin, sprinkle with salt and pepper, then roast in the centre of the oven for 15 minutes on each side. Meanwhile, put the honey, soy sauce, ketchup and garlic in a heatproof bowl. Add the water and stock cube and stir until dissolved. Pour over the chops, then turn the oven down to medium temperature and continue roasting for a further 30 minutes or until the chops are tender. Baste occasionally with the sauce and turn the chops over during cooking. Mix the cornflour to a paste with a little water. Transfer the roasting tin to the top of the stove, stir in the cornflour paste, then cook until the sauce thickens, stirring constantly. Taste and adjust the seasoning, then serve hot with seasonal vegetables.

Somerset chicken

Metric
1 large knob of butter
1 large onion, peeled
*   and finely chopped*
4 chicken portions, skinned
salt
freshly ground black pepper
2 × 15 ml spoons flour
300 ml dry cider
150 ml water
1 × 5 ml spoon dried mixed
*   or fresh herbs*
1 × 275 g can carrots,
*   drained and sliced*

Imperial
1 large knob of butter
1 large onion, peeled
*   and finely chopped*
4 chicken portions, skinned
salt
freshly ground black pepper
2 tablespoons flour
½ pint dry cider
¼ pint water
1 teaspoon dried mixed
*   or fresh herbs*
1 × 10 oz can carrots,
*   drained and sliced*

Somerset chicken

Oven cooking time: 1¼ hours

Melt the butter in a flameproof casserole dish, add the onion and fry over gentle heat until soft. Meanwhile, sprinkle the chicken with salt and pepper, then coat in the flour. Add the chicken to the casserole and fry until browned on both sides.

Preheat the oven at medium temperature for 5 minutes. Stir the cider and water into the casserole, then add the herbs and bring to the boil. Cover, then transfer to the centre of the oven and cook for 1¼ hours or until the chicken is tender. Add the carrots for the last 10 minutes of cooking time. Taste and adjust the seasoning, then serve straight from the casserole with boiled or mashed potatoes and a seasonal green vegetable.

Variations:
Substitute sliced mushrooms or drained, canned sweetcorn for the carrots.

Apple batter pudding

Metric
12 × 15 ml spoons
  flour
1 egg, beaten
300 ml milk
1 knob of butter or lard
2 large cooking apples
4 × 15 ml spoons sugar
1 × 5 ml spoon ground
  cinnamon

Imperial
12 tablespoons
  flour
1 egg, beaten
½ pint milk
1 knob of butter or lard
2 large cooking apples
4 tablespoons sugar
1 teaspoon ground
  cinnamon

Oven cooking time: 15–20 minutes

Put the flour in the bowl, make a well in the centre, then add the egg and half the milk. Beat well, then gradually beat in the remaining milk. Preheat the oven at high temperature for 5 minutes. Put the butter or lard in a large shallow baking tin, then heat in the centre of the oven for about 5 minutes or until smoking hot. Meanwhile, peel, core and slice the apples thinly. When the fat is hot, arrange the apples evenly in the bottom of the tin, sprinkle with the sugar and cinnamon, then pour over the batter. Return to the oven and bake for 15 to 20 minutes until risen and crisp. Serve immediately with fresh pouring cream.

Sweet Indian rice

Metric
3 × 15 ml spoons pudding
  rice
2 × 15 ml spoons seedless
  raisins
2 × 15 ml spoons flaked
  blanched almonds
2 × 15 ml spoons honey
2 × 15 ml spoons sugar, or
  to taste
600 ml milk
1 × 2.5 ml spoon ground
  mixed spice or cinnamon
1 knob of butter

Imperial
3 tablespoons pudding
  rice
2 tablespoons seedless
  raisins
2 tablespoons flaked
  blanched almonds
2 tablespoons honey
2 tablespoons sugar, or
  to taste
1 pint milk
½ teaspoon ground
  mixed spice or cinnamon
1 knob of butter

Oven cooking time: 1 hour

Preheat the oven at high temperature for 5 minutes. Put all the ingredients in an ovenproof dish, then bake in the centre of the oven for 30 minutes. Lower the temperature to medium, transfer the dish to the floor of the oven and continue cooking for a further 30 minutes or until the rice is tender.

Mincemeat jalousie

Metric	Imperial
1 × 400 g packet frozen puff pastry, thawed	1 × 14 oz packet frozen puff pastry, thawed
6 × 15 ml spoons mincemeat	6 tablespoons mincemeat
1 small egg, beaten	1 small egg, beaten
2 × 15 ml spoons sugar	2 tablespoons sugar
1 × 5 ml spoon ground cinnamon	1 teaspoon ground cinnamon

Oven cooking time: about 25 minutes

Cut the pastry in two, then roll out each piece to an oblong about 25 × 15 cm/10 × 6 inches. Place one piece of pastry on a baking sheet and spread the mincemeat over it, leaving a 2.5 cm/1 in margin around the edges.

Preheat the oven at high temperature for 5 minutes. Place the remaining piece of pastry over the mincemeat, brush the edges with water, then press together and flute them to seal. Brush all over the pastry with the egg, then cut diagonal slits in the top piece of pastry. Sprinkle with the sugar and cinnamon, then bake in the centre of the oven for about 25 minutes. Turn the baking sheet round half way through cooking, and cover the pastry with foil if it is becoming too brown. Leave to stand for 5 minutes before serving as a dessert with fresh cream. Or leave until cold, then slice thinly and serve as a tea time treat.

Variations:
Substitute jam or lemon curd for the mincemeat, or 2 peeled, cored and sliced cooking apples, sprinkled with sugar to taste.

Rhubarb and ginger betty

Metric	Imperial
750 g rhubarb, trimmed and cut into small chunks	1½ lb rhubarb, trimmed and cut into small chunks
6 × 15 ml spoons brown sugar	6 tablespoons brown sugar
finely grated rind and juice of 1 large orange	finely grated rind and juice of 1 large orange
1 × 2.5 ml spoon ground ginger	½ teaspoon ground ginger
1 small loaf, crusts removed	1 small loaf, crusts removed
2 knobs of butter	2 knobs of butter

Oven cooking time: 40 minutes

Preheat the oven at medium temperature for 5 minutes. Put half the rhubarb in the bottom of a baking tin, then sprinkle over half the sugar, orange rind and juice and ginger. Crumble half the bread over the mixture, then repeat these layers once more. Dot with the butter, then bake in the centre of the oven for 20 minutes. Increase the temperature to high, then bake for a further 20 minutes. Serve hot or cold with cream or ice cream.

Variations:
Use halved and stoned plums, or peeled, cored and sliced apples instead of the rhubarb, and substitute cinnamon for the ginger.

From left: Mincemeat jalousie; Rhubarb and ginger betty; Sweet Indian rice; Apple batter pudding

79

COLD & NO-COOK DISHES

There will always be times on holiday when you simply don't feel like cooking, or the weather is too hot, or you've simply run out of gas! At such times you will obviously not want to spend much time preparing cold meals, so the recipes in this chapter have been kept deliberately simple, and most of them require no cooking at all. This is also particularly important when it comes to desserts, because it is very rare that you will have any free burners at the same time as you are cooking the main course. If you are lucky enough to have a camping refrigerator, then obviously cold desserts will be less of a problem, although it is possible to make most of the desserts in this chapter without one. Don't forget that you can also take most of these dishes on picnics: pack them in rigid polythene containers and carry them in a cool box if you have one.

Tuna fish salad

Metric	Imperial
2 × 225 g cans tuna, drained and flaked	2 × 8 oz cans tuna, drained and flaked
1 large green pepper, cored, seeded and sliced	1 large green pepper, cored, seeded and sliced
½ large cucumber, peeled and diced	½ large cucumber, peeled and diced
3 firm tomatoes, chopped	3 firm tomatoes, chopped
juice of ½ lemon	juice of ½ lemon
4 × 15 ml spoons bottled mayonnaise	4 tablespoons bottled mayonnaise
salt	salt
freshly ground black pepper	freshly ground black pepper

Put the tuna, green pepper, cucumber and tomatoes in a bowl, sprinkle with the lemon juice and stir gently to mix. Fold in the mayonnaise with salt and pepper to taste. Serve on a bed of lettuce and garnish with tomato quarters, if liked.

Variation:
Substitute 150 ml/¼ pint oil and vinegar dressing for the mayonnaise.

Potato salad

Metric	Imperial
1 kg new potatoes, scrubbed and halved	2 lb new potatoes, scrubbed and halved
salt	salt
1 small Spanish onion, peeled and very finely chopped	1 small Spanish onion, peeled and very finely chopped
4 × 15 ml spoons bottled mayonnaise	4 tablespoons bottled mayonnaise
4 × 15 ml spoons plain unsweetened yogurt	4 tablespoons plain unsweetened yogurt
freshly ground black pepper	freshly ground black pepper

Cook the potatoes in boiling salted water for about 15 minutes or until just tender, then drain. Cover in cold water for 5 minutes, then drain again. Leave until completely cold, then slice or cut into small chunks. Put the potatoes in a bowl with the remaining ingredients and salt and pepper to taste, then fold gently together until well mixed.

Variations:
Substitute 2 × 500 g/1 lb cans new potatoes, drained and sliced, for the fresh potatoes. If available, chopped parsley, chives or green pepper will add colour and extra flavour.

Mackerel spread

Metric	Imperial
1 × 225 g mackerel fillets in tomato sauce, drained	1 × 8 oz can mackerel fillets in tomato sauce, drained
juice of ½ lemon	juice of ½ lemon
3 × 15 ml spoons bottled mayonnaise	3 tablespoons bottled mayonnaise
2 × 5 ml spoons horseradish cream	2 teaspoons horseradish cream
freshly ground black pepper	freshly ground black pepper

Put all the ingredients in a bowl with plenty of pepper and beat together until smooth. Spoon into a polythene container and smooth the top. Cover and chill for at least 1 hour. Serve with crusty French bread and butter, crispbreads or crackers.

Potato salad; Mackerel spread; Tuna fish salad

Salad niçoise

Metric	Imperial
1 bunch of watercress	1 bunch of watercress
1 large lettuce heart, quartered	1 large lettuce heart, quartered
4 tomatoes, quartered	4 tomatoes, quartered
3 hard-boiled eggs, quartered	3 hard-boiled eggs, quartered
1 × 50 g can anchovies, drained	1 × 2 oz can anchovies, drained
6 × 15 ml spoons olive oil	6 tablespoons olive oil
2 × 15 ml spoons wine vinegar or lemon juice	2 tablespoons wine vinegar or lemon juice
1 × 2.5 ml spoon prepared French mustard	½ teaspoon prepared French mustard
salt	salt
freshly ground black pepper	freshly ground black pepper

Arrange the sprigs of watercress around the outside of a salad bowl, then place the lettuce and tomatoes in the centre, with the hard-boiled eggs and anchovies on top. Put the remaining ingredients in a jug with salt and pepper to taste. Beat until well mixed, then pour over the salad just before serving.

Variations :
Add 1 × 200 g/7 oz can tuna, drained and flaked, or 1 × 100 g/4 oz can sardines in oil, drained. Or vary the salad vegetables according to availability – add celery, green and red peppers, fennel, spring onions, radishes, etc.
Pitted black olives can also be added to make a classic salad niçoise.

Below: Salad niçoise

Gazpacho

Metric	Imperial
1 × 400 g can tomatoes	1 × 14 oz can tomatoes
2 slices of bread, crusts removed	2 slices of bread, crusts removed
½ small Spanish onion, peeled and very finely chopped	½ small Spanish onion, peeled and very finely chopped
2 green peppers, cored, seeded and very finely chopped	2 green peppers, cored, seeded and very finely chopped
2 garlic cloves, peeled and crushed	2 garlic cloves, peeled and crushed
3 × 15 ml spoons olive oil	3 tablespoons olive oil
3 × 15 ml spoons wine vinegar	3 tablespoons wine vinegar
300 ml water	½ pint water
1 × 2.5 ml spoon sugar	½ teaspoon sugar
salt	salt
freshly ground black pepper	freshly ground black pepper
½ cucumber, very finely chopped, to finish	½ cucumber, very finely chopped, to finish

Use an automatic chopper for the onion, peppers and cucumber, if you have one.

Work the canned tomatoes through a fine wire sieve into a bowl. Grate or crumble the bread into the bowl, then stir in the remaining ingredients, except the cucumber, with salt and pepper to taste. Chill for several hours, stirring occasionally, then taste and adjust the seasoning. Sprinkle the cucumber over the soup just before serving.

Quick egg mayonnaise

Metric	Imperial
8 lettuce leaves	8 lettuce leaves
4 tomatoes, sliced	4 tomatoes, sliced
salt	salt
freshly ground black pepper	freshly ground black pepper
4 hard-boiled eggs, halved lengthways	4 hard-boiled eggs, halved lengthways
8 × 15 ml spoons bottled mayonnaise	8 tablespoons bottled mayonnaise
cress, to garnish	cress, to garnish

Put the lettuce leaves around the edge of a large dish. Arrange the tomato slices on top and sprinkle with salt and pepper. Arrange the egg halves cut side down in the centre. Spoon over the mayonnaise, sprinkle with more salt and pepper, garnish with cress and serve with bread and butter.

Right: Quick egg mayonnaise; Gazpacho

Liver sausage pâté

Metric	Imperial
225 g liver sausage	½ lb liver sausage
100 g cream cheese and chives	4 oz cream cheese and chives
50 g butter, softened	2 oz butter, softened
2 × 15 ml spoons milk	2 tablespoons milk
freshly ground black pepper	freshly ground black pepper

Put all the ingredients in a bowl with pepper to taste, then beat well to mix. Press the mixture into a well buttered polythene container and smooth the top. Cover and chill for several hours or overnight if possible, then turn out to serve, if liked. Serve with crusty French bread and butter.
Serves 6

Variation:
If you happen to have a bottle of wine, sherry or brandy or dry cider open, then substitute 2 × 15 ml spoons/2 tablespoons for the milk.

Rice salad

Metric	Imperial
225 g long-grain rice, boiled and drained	½ lb long-grain rice, boiled and drained
1 small onion, peeled and finely chopped	1 small onion, peeled and finely chopped
1 green pepper, cored, seeded and finely chopped	1 green pepper, cored, seeded and finely chopped
1 red pepper, cored, seeded and finely chopped	1 red pepper, cored, seeded and finely chopped
4 × 15 ml spoons chopped nuts (almonds, cashews, peanuts, walnuts)	4 tablespoons chopped nuts (almonds, cashews, peanuts, walnuts)
4 × 15 ml spoons bottled mayonnaise	4 tablespoons bottled mayonnaise
salt	salt
freshly ground black pepper	freshly ground black pepper

Put all the ingredients in a bowl with salt and pepper to taste, then stir well to mix.

Variations:
Substitute 1 × 225 g/8 oz can sweetcorn and peppers (drained) for the green and red peppers. Or substitute 1 × 50 g/2 oz packet nuts and raisins for the nuts.
Add chopped ham or luncheon meat to serve as a main course salad. If preferred, use a French dressing instead of the mayonnaise.

Sardine salad

Metric	Imperial
2 eating apples	2 eating apples
juice of ½ lemon	juice of ½ lemon
75 g Edam or Gouda cheese, diced	3 oz Edam or Gouda cheese, diced
1 handful of broken walnuts, finely chopped	1 handful of broken walnuts, finely chopped
1 × 150 ml carton soured cream	1 × 5 fl oz carton soured cream
salt	salt
freshly ground black pepper	freshly ground black pepper
8 lettuce leaves	8 lettuce leaves
2 × 100 g cans sardines in oil, drained	2 × 4 oz cans sardines in oil, drained
sprig of parsley, to garnish	sprig of parsley, to garnish

Peel and core the apples, then chop finely. Put in a bowl and sprinkle with a little lemon juice, then add the cheese, walnuts, half the soured cream and salt and pepper to taste. Stir well to mix. Arrange the letture leaves in a circle on a large plate or dish, then spoon the apple and cheese mixture on top. Arrange the sardines in a circle and sprinkle with the remaining lemon juice. Spoon the remaining soured cream in the centre of the sardines and garnish with parsley.

Variation:
Any canned fish in oil can be used instead of the sardines – try mackerel, brisling or pilchards.

From front: Liver sausage pâté; Rice salad; Sardine salad

Russian salad

Metric
1 × 225 g packet frozen
    mixed vegetables with
    sweetcorn
4 small beetroot
1 × 500 g can new
    potatoes, drained and
    chopped
1 × 150 ml carton soured
    cream
3 × 15 ml spoons bottled
    mayonnaise
1 × 15 ml spoon creamed
    horseradish or prepared
    mustard (optional)
salt
freshly ground black pepper

Imperial
1 × 8 oz packet frozen
    mixed vegetables with
    sweetcorn
4 small beetroot
1 × 1 lb can new
    potatoes, drained and
    chopped
1 × 5 fl oz carton soured
    cream
3 tablespoons bottled
    mayonnaise
1 teaspoon creamed
    horseradish or prepared
    mustard (optional)
salt
freshly ground black pepper

Cook the mixed vegetables according to packet directions, then drain thoroughly and leave to cool. Chop half the beetroot, then put in a bowl with the mixed vegetables and potatoes. Add half the soured cream, the mayonnaise, horseradish or mustard (if using) and salt and pepper to taste.

Fold gently until well mixed. Slice the remaining beetroot and arrange in a circle on top of the salad. Spoon the remaining soured cream in the centre. Serve with cold cooked meats.
Serves 6

Variations:
Boiled new potatoes can be substituted for the canned potatoes – the flavour will be better, but the preparation time considerably longer.
Chopped or sliced cooked meat can be added to the salad to make it more substantial.

Potted salmon

86

Spicy mushroom salad; Russian salad

Potted salmon

Metric	Imperial
1 × 200 g can salmon, drained	1 × 7 oz can salmon, drained
1 × 225 g carton cottage cheese with chives	1 × 8 oz carton cottage cheese with chives
2 × 15 ml spoons bottled mayonnaise	2 tablespoons bottled mayonnaise
2 × 15 ml spoons Worcestershire sauce	2 tablespoons Worcestershire sauce
freshly ground black pepper	freshly ground black pepper

Put all the ingredients in a bowl with pepper to taste, then beat well to mix. Spoon the mixture into a polythene container and smooth the top. Cover and chill for several hours or overnight if possible. Serve as a spread with crackers, crispbreads, toast or French bread.
Serves 6 to 8

Variation:
Substitute cream cheese for the cottage cheese to make a smoother spread.

Spicy mushroom salad

Metric	Imperial
1 × 15 ml spoons Worcestershire sauce	1 tablespoon Worcestershire sauce
1 × 1.25 ml spoon prepared French mustard	¼ teaspoon prepared French mustard
juice of ½ lemon	juice of ½ lemon
2 × 15 ml spoons oil	2 tablespoons oil
225 g button mushrooms, finely sliced	½ lb button mushrooms, finely sliced
freshly ground black pepper	freshly ground black pepper

If available, chopped chives or parsley give colour and flavour to this salad.

Put the Worcestershire sauce, mustard, lemon juice and oil in a bowl and beat well to mix. Add the mushrooms and stir until thoroughly coated in the dressing, then add pepper to taste. Leave to stand for about 30 minutes, stirring occasionally.

Peach melba; Chocolate mousse

Chocolate mousse

Metric
1 × 100 g bar plain
  chocolate, broken up
1 × 150 g packet
  marshmallows
4 × 15 ml spoons milk
2 eggs, separated
1 × 150 ml carton double
  cream, stiffly whipped
grated chocolate, to
  decorate

Imperial
1 × 4 oz bar plain
  chocolate, broken up
1 × 5 oz packet
  marshmallows
4 tablespoons milk
2 eggs, separated
1 × 5 fl oz carton double
  cream, stiffly whipped
grated chocolate, to
  decorate

Put the chocolate, marshmallows and milk in a pan and melt over a gentle heat, stirring occasionally. Leave to cool for 5 minutes, then stir in the egg yolks. Leave until completely cold, then stir in the cream reserving some for decoration. Beat the egg whites until stiff, then fold into the mousse until evenly blended. Spoon into individual dishes, then top with a blob of cream and sprinkle over the grated chocolate. Chill in the refrigerator until set.
Serves 6

Sweet summer flan

Metric
225 g fresh raspberries
50 g sugar, or to taste
1 × 150 ml carton double
  or whipping cream
1 × 150 ml carton single
  cream
1 small sponge flan case

Imperial
½ lb fresh raspberries
2 oz sugar, or to taste
1 × 5 fl oz carton double
  or whipping cream
1 × 5 fl oz carton single
  cream
1 small sponge flan case

Chop the raspberries, reserving a few whole ones for decoration. Put the chopped raspberries and sugar in a bowl, stir gently to mix, then leave for 5 to 10 minutes. Meanwhile, put the creams together in a separate bowl and beat until thick. Fold in the chopped raspberries, then spread in the flan case. Use the whole raspberries to decorate the top of the flan. Keep in a cool place until serving time.

Variations:
Any fresh fruit can be used instead of the raspberries – try hulled strawberries, stoned cherries or peaches.

Sweet summer flan; Lemonade

Peach melba

Metric
1 × 200 g can raspberries
2 × 15 ml spoons icing
  sugar
1 × 5 ml spoon arrowroot
  or cornflour
1 × 15 ml spoon water
1 × 300 ml carton vanilla
  ice cream
4 fresh peaches, skinned,
  halved and stoned

Imperial
1 × 7 oz can raspberries
2 tablespoons icing
  sugar
1 teaspoon arrowroot
  or cornflour
1 tablespoon water
1 × 10 fl oz carton vanilla
  ice cream
4 fresh peaches, skinned,
  halved and stoned

Work the raspberries through a sieve into a small pan. Stir in the icing sugar. Mix the arrowroot or corn-flour to a paste with the water, then stir into the pan. Bring to the boil, stirring constantly, then simmer for 1 to 2 minutes until thick and glossy. Leave to cool. Divide the ice cream equally between 4 individual bowls, then arrange two peach halves on either side of the ice cream. Pour over the sauce and serve immediately.

Lemonade

Metric
3 lemons, halved
1¾ litres water
500 g sugar, or to taste
2 × 15 ml spoons citric acid

Imperial
3 lemons, halved
3 pints water
1 lb sugar, or to taste
2 tablespoons citric acid

Squeeze the lemons and set the juice aside. Cut the lemon skins into thick slices, then put in a pan with the water. Bring to the boil, remove from the heat and add the lemon juice, sugar and citric acid. Stir to dissolve the sugar, then leave to cool. Strain into a jug, cover and chill in the refrigerator.
Serve diluted with water to taste. Use within 1 week if kept in the refrigerator, or 1 to 2 days if kept at cool room temperature.
Makes 1¾ litres/3 pints

Cherry cheesecake

Metric
1 × 200 g packet ginger
 biscuits
100 g butter or margarine,
 melted
1 × 300 ml carton double
 cream
4 × 15 ml spoons icing
 sugar
225 g cream cheese
1 × 400 g can cherry pie
 filling

Imperial
1 × 7 oz packet ginger
 biscuits
4 oz butter or margarine,
 melted
1 × 10 fl oz carton double
 cream
4 tablespoons icing
 sugar
½ lb cream cheese
1 × 14 oz can cherry pie
 filling

Put the biscuits in a bowl and crush to fine crumbs with the end of a rolling pin. Add the melted butter or margarine and stir well to mix. Press the mixture into the bottom and sides of a 20 cm/8 in flan dish, then chill for about 30 minutes until firm.
Beat the cream until thick, then beat in the icing sugar and cream cheese until well blended. Spread the mixture over the base of the flan. Spread the pie filling on top to cover the cream mixture completely. Chill until serving time.
Serves 6

Variations :
Use any kind of pie filling, or use fresh fruit such as stoned cherries, seedless grapes, sliced bananas, halved strawberries or whole raspberries – and sprinkle with sugar to taste.

Yogurt jelly; Whipped pears

Cherry cheesecake

Whipped pears

Metric	Imperial
1 × 400 g can pear halves	1 × 14 oz can pear halves
1 × 25 g packet yellow jelly glaze	1 × 1 oz packet yellow jelly glaze
200 ml water	⅓ pint water
1 × 150 ml carton double cream, stiffly whipped	1 × 5 fl oz carton double cream, stiffly whipped
2 egg whites, stiffly whipped	2 egg whites, stiffly whipped
2 × 15 ml spoons flaked almonds, to decorate (optional)	2 tablespoons flaked almonds, to decorate (optional)

Mash the pears and juice to a purée with a fork, set aside. Put the jelly glaze powder and water in a pan and stir to dissolve. Bring to the boil, stirring contantly, then remove from the heat and beat until thick and glossy. Beat into the pear purée until evenly blended, then beat in the cream. Fold in the egg whites until evenly blended, then leave in a cool place or chill in the refrigerator until set. Sprinkle with the almonds (if using) just before serving.
Serves 6

Variations:
Any kind of canned fruit can be substituted for the pears.
If liked, use a larger can of fruit and reserve a few pieces of fruit to decorate the top of the dessert before mashing the remainder.

Yogurt jelly

Metric	Imperial
1 × 100 g packet blackcurrant flavour jelly	1 × 4 oz packet blackcurrant flavour jelly
1 small carton black cherry yogurt	1 small carton black cherry yogurt
2 × 15 ml spoons honey (optional)	2 tablespoons honey (optional)

Dissolve the jelly in 300 ml/½ pint boiling water according to packet directions. Stir in 150 ml/¼ pint cold water, then leave to cool.
Add the yogurt and honey (if using) and beat for a few minutes until well mixed. Chill for several hours or overnight until set. Serve with whipped cream, or chop the jelly roughly and serve in individual bowls with ice cream for the children.
Serves 4 to 6

Variations:
Any combination of flavours can be used according to taste – try raspberry or strawberry jelly with the same flavour yogurt.
For a richer, creamier dessert, add 150 ml/¼ pint whipped cream to the jelly with the yogurt.
For a lighter version, use a large (500 g/1 lb) carton of yogurt instead of the small one.

Chocolate refrigerator cake

Metric	Imperial
1 × 100 g bar plain chocolate, broken up	1 × 4 oz bar plain chocolate, broken up
100 g unsalted butter	4 oz unsalted butter
5 × 15 ml spoons golden syrup	5 tablespoons golden syrup
1 × 225 g packet rich tea biscuits	1 × 8 oz packet rich tea biscuits
2 × 15 ml spoons chopped nuts	2 tablespoons chopped nuts
2 × 15 ml spoons chopped glacé cherries	2 tablespoons chopped glacé cherries

Put the chocolate, butter and golden syrup in a pan and heat gently until melted, stirring occasionally. Meanwhile, put the biscuits in a bowl and crush to fine crumbs with the end of a rolling pin. Add the melted mixture, nuts and cherries and stir well to mix. Line the base of a small non-stick pan with silver foil. Press the mixture into the pan, then chill in the refrigerator overnight. Turn out, remove the foil, then cut into thin slices to serve.
Makes about 12 slices

Blackberry mousse

Metric	Imperial
1 × 100 g packet blackcurrant jelly	1 × 4 oz packet blackcurrant jelly
300 ml boiling water	½ pint boiling water
500 g fresh blackberries	1 lb fresh blackberries
4 × 15 ml spoons sugar	4 tablespoons sugar
2 egg whites, stiffly whipped	2 egg whites, stiffly whipped
To decorate:	To decorate:
fresh blackberries	fresh blackberries
sugar	sugar

Dissolve the jelly in the boiling water, then set aside. Put the blackberries and sugar in a pan and heat gently for 10 minutes until soft, stirring occasionally. Stir into the jelly, then leave in a cool place until just beginning to set.
Fold the egg whites into the blackberry mixture until evenly blended. Leave in a cool place or chill in the refrigerator until set. Decorate with fresh blackberries and sprinkle with sugar before serving.
Serves 6

Banana boats

Metric	Imperial
1 × 50 g bar plain chocolate, broken into pieces	1 × 2 oz bar plain chocolate, broken into pieces
2 × 15 ml spoons water	2 tablespoons water
1 × 150 ml carton double cream	1 × 5 fl oz carton double cream
1 × 300 ml carton vanilla ice cream	1 × 10 fl oz carton vanilla ice cream
4 bananas	4 bananas
2 × 15 ml spoons chopped nuts	2 tablespoons chopped nuts

Put the chocolate and water in a non-stick pan and heat gently until melted, stirring occasionally. Remove from the heat, leave to cool slightly, then stir in half the cream. Beat the remaining cream until stiff. Slice the bananas in two lengthways, then place in individual shallow bowls. Top with scoops of ice cream, then drizzle over the melted chocolate. Top each boat with whipped cream, then sprinkle with nuts. Serve immediately.

Variation:
For a less expensive version, omit the fresh cream.

Ginger meringue nests

Metric	Imperial
6 × 15 ml spoons ginger marmalade	6 tablespoons ginger marmalade
1 × 15 ml spoon undiluted orange squash	1 tablespoon undiluted orange squash
6 meringue nests	6 meringue nests
6 scoops of vanilla ice cream	6 scoops of vanilla ice cream
fresh pouring cream, to serve	fresh pouring cream, to serve

Put the marmalade and orange squash in a pan and heat gently until melted, stirring occasionally. Leave to cool. Put the meringues in individual serving bowls, then put one scoop of ice cream in each. Pour the sauce over the ice cream, then serve immediately with fresh pouring cream handed separately.
Serves 6

Ginger meringue nests; Chocolate refrigerator cake; Blackberry mousse; Banana boats

Sweet sauces for ice cream
Strawberry sauce

Metric	Imperial
1 × 200 g can strawberries	1 × 7 oz can strawberries
150 ml water	¼ pint water
juice of ½ lemon	juice of ½ lemon
2 × 5 ml spoons arrowroot	2 teaspoons arrowroot

Work the strawberries and juice through a sieve into a pan. Stir in the water and lemon juice, then heat through to boiling point. Mix the arrowroot to a paste with a little water, then add to the pan and simmer until the sauce thickens, stirring constantly. Leave to cool before pouring over the ice cream.

Chocolate nut sauce

Metric	Imperial
1 × 50 g bar plain chocolate, broken into pieces	1 × 2 oz bar plain chocolate, broken into pieces
1 knob of butter	1 knob of butter
1 × 15 ml spoon golden syrup	1 tablespoon golden syrup
2 × 15 ml spoons icing sugar	2 tablespoons icing sugar
2 × 15 ml spoons cold water	2 tablespoons cold water
2 × 15 ml spoons chopped mixed nuts	2 tablespoons chopped mixed nuts

Put the chocolate, butter and syrup in a pan and heat gently until melted, stirring occasionally. Sprinkle in the icing sugar and beat until smooth, then remove from the heat and stir in the water and nuts. Leave to stand for 10 minutes before pouring over ice cream.

Camper's trifle

Metric	Imperial
6 trifle sponges, cut in half	6 trifle sponges, cut in half
4 × 15 ml spoons jam, for spreading	4 tablespoons jam, for spreading
2 × 300 g cans mandarin oranges	2 × 11 oz can mandarin oranges
1 × 100 g packet orange jelly	1 × 4 oz packet orange jelly
1 × 75 g packet instant custard mix	1 × 3 oz packet instant custard mix
1 × 150 ml carton double or whipping cream, stiffly whipped	1 × 5 fl oz carton double or whipping cream, stiffly whipped

Spread the sponges with the jam, sandwich them together and place in the bottom of a deep serving bowl. Drain the mandarins and reserve the juice. Dissolve the jelly in 300 ml/½ pint boiling water according to packet directions, then stir in enough mandarin juice to make up to 600 ml/1 pint. Pour over the sponge cakes, add half the mandarins and chill until set.
Put the custard mix in a measuring jug, then add boiling water to come up to the 300 ml/½ pint mark. Stir briskly to make a thick custard. Leave to cool slightly, then spread over the set jelly. Leave until cold, then spread the cream on top. Decorate with the remaining mandarins.
Serves 6 to 8

Variations:
Substitute canned apricot halves or sliced peaches for the mandarins and use a different flavour jelly if liked. If you have any sherry or sweet white wine, pour a few spoonfuls over the sponge cakes before adding the jelly.

Camper's trifle; Chocolate nut sauce; Strawberry sauce

Index

PDO 81-843